STATE OF HEALTH SERIES

Edited by Chris Ham, Director of Health Services Management
Centre, University of Birmingham

ACCREDITATION
Protecting the Professional or the Consumer?

Ellie Scrivens

Open University Press
Buckingham · Philadelphia

PN
11623

Open University Press
Celtic Court
22 Ballmoor
Buckingham
MK18 1XW

and
1900 Frost Road, Suite 101
Bristol, PA 19007, USA

First Published 1995

A catalogue record of this book is available from the British Library

ISBN 0 335 19492 3 (hb)   0 335 19491 5 (pb)

Library of Congress Cataloging-in-Publication Data

Scrivens, Ellie, 1954–
    Accreditation: protecting the professional or the consumer?/Ellie
Scrivens.
    p.   cm. — (State of health series)
Includes bibliographical references and index.
ISBN 0-335-19492-3 (hb)   ISBN 0-335-19491-5 (pbk)
—Accreditation—Great Britain.   I. Title.   II. Series.
RA965.8S37 1995   94-44778
362.1'021841–dc20   CIP

WP 21
ACCREDITATION
Q A   HEALTH CARE
        HEALTH SERVICES
                NHS
CONSUMER
    SATISFACTION

Typeset by Type Study, Scarborough, North Yorkshire
Printed in Great Britain by St Edmundsbury Press,
Bury St Edmunds, Suffolk

For David and Kester

CONTENTS

SERIES EDITOR'S INTRODUCTION

Health services in many developed countries have come under critical scrutiny in recent years. In part this is because of increasing expenditure, much of it funded from public sources, and the pressure this has put on governments seeking to control public spending. Also important has been the perception that resources allocated to health services are not always deployed in an optimal fashion. Thus at a time when the scope for increasing expenditure is extremely limited, there is a need to search for ways of using existing budgets more efficiently. A further concern has been the desire to ensure access to health care of various groups on an equitable basis. In some countries this has been linked to a wish to enhance patient choice and to make service providers more responsive to patients as 'consumers'.

Underlying these specific concerns are a number of more fundamental developments which have a significant bearing on the performance of health services. Three are worth highlighting. First, there are demographic changes, including the ageing population and the decline in the proportion of the population of working age. These changes will both increase the demand for health care and at the same time limit the ability of health services to respond to this demand.

Second, advances in medical science will also give rise to new demands within the health services. These advances cover a range of possibilities, including innovations in surgery, drug therapy, screening and diagnosis. The pace of innovation is likely to quicken as the end of the century approaches, with significant implications for the funding and provision of services.

Third, public expectations of health services are rising as those who use services demand higher standards of care. In part, this is stimulated by developments within the health service, including the availability of new technology. More fundamentally, it stems from the emergence of a more educated and informed population, in which people are accustomed to being treated as consumers rather than patients.

Against this background, policymakers in a number of countries are reviewing the future of health services. Those countries which have traditionally relied on a market in health care are making greater use of regulation and planning. Equally, those countries which have traditionally relied on regulation and planning are moving towards a more competitive approach. In no country is there complete satisfaction with existing methods of financing and delivery, and everywhere there is a search for new policy instruments.

The aim of this series is to contribute to debate about the future of health services through an analysis of major issues in health policy. These issues have been chosen because they are both of current interest and of enduring importance. The series is intended to be accessible to students and informed lay readers as well as to specialists working in this field. The aim is to go beyond a textbook approach to health policy analysis and to encourage authors to move debate about their issue forward. In this sense, each book presents a summary of current research and thinking, and an exploration of future policy directions.

Professor Chris Ham
Director of Health Services Management Centre,
University of Birmingham

PREFACE

The Department of Health commissioned the study upon which this book is based. The views expressed here are those of the author and not the Department of Health. The aim of the research was to ascertain the ins and outs of accreditation and I am grateful to them for their assistance, especially Anne Kauder who was our research liaison officer. The research was divided into eight stages. First, to understand and describe the processes of accreditation by looking at the international picture. Second, to map the existing accreditation activities in England and to compare them. Third, to ascertain the views of purchasers and providers about accreditation as a system of quality control. Fourth, to examine the implementation of one particular accreditation system, the King's Fund Organisational Audit, in depth. Fifth, to develop a means of costing the impact of an accreditation system upon a hospital. Sixth, the former South East Thames Regional Health Authority, in conjunction with the Department of Health funded a separate study of a new accreditation system. Seven, to make recommendations about the way forward for accreditation. Eight, to identify areas for future research.

I should like to thank the researchers from Keele University and the University of Bath, who worked on this study with enormous enthusiasm and dedication. Without their energy and support, the work could not have been completed in the incredibly short space of time we were allotted. They are Sharon Redmayne who was responsible for the interviews at one of the two hospital sites who underwent the King's Fund Organisational Audit, and for the analysis of the questionnaire data. Lindsay St. Clair who was responsible for the study of the second King's Fund hospital site. Andrea Steiner who undertook background research into developments in the USA and interviews with Chief Executives around England, finding out their views and opinions on accreditation. Jane Springham who studied the development of an accreditation system in South East Thames (later to be South Thames) Regional Health Authority. Sue Nancholas conducted the interviews with the managers of the community hospitals in South Western Regional Health Authority. Kevin Hunt, and Marilyn James of the Centre for Health Planning and Management at Keele University, who studied the costing issues involved in accreditation. Louise Hussey coordinated the research work and kept us all on track. The work which contributed to this book is presented in more detail in working papers produced from the Centre for Health Planning and Management at Keele University.

My greatest thanks go to Rudolf Klein, Professor of Social Policy at Bath University, without whose insights and invaluable contribution the report would be all the poorer and who helped greatly with Chapter 1. My thanks must also go to Dr Karin Von Degenberg from the NHS Executive, whose support and infectious enthusiasm for the topic of accreditation and quality assurance added to the interest of the study.

My thanks also go to Gillian Dalley of South Thames Region who organized this part of the research. The work in South Western was funded by the South Western Community Hospitals accreditation scheme, and my thanks go to Jackie Hayes for all her help and support.

And my final thanks must go to all the people who helped us to understand the processes of accreditation and its impact on health care. Some I cannot name – in the hospital interviews we promised anonymity to respondents, but my debt to them for their time and patience is enormous. I should like to thank in particular, Avril Toland of The Royal Hospital in Chesterfield in Derbyshire and David Pokora from the Princess Margaret Hospital of the Swindon and Marlborough NHS Trust who gave me insight into quality control and assurance including their own experiences as surveyors for the King's Fund. In addition, Tessa Brooks from the King's Fund Organisational Audit, Charles Shaw from CASPE who masterminded the South Western Regional Health Authority accreditation scheme, Brian Edwards of West Midlands Region, Reynold Tarkinter and Mike Miller who introduced me to standards in estate management and managers from Sunderland and Trent who widened my horizons on the applicability of accreditation in health care and all the many people who gave us their time and opinions. I should also like to thank colleagues in other countries who explained the details of their accreditation systems. Bill Jesse from the Joint Commission, Elma Heidemann from the Canadian Council, Lluis Bohigas and Ulises Ruiz who explained the Spanish system and Robert Reznik from Australia.

INTRODUCTION

Politicians are becoming increasingly worried about whether health services are providing value for money. Consumers are worried about whether they will be able to receive the health care which they need, when they need it. Everyone is worried that professionals may not be acting in the best interests of patients. But more significantly, deep down, we are all worried that the health services which treat us when we are ill just might be causing more damage than good. How do we know that hospitals are not employing unqualified doctors, using the wrong equipment, producing the wrong medical record when we are on the operating table? There is no way of telling except by ensuring that the hospital got it right in the first place. And at the moment we have only one way of finding out – by asking if the hospital is properly run.

This is a discussion of the issues raised by approaches to monitoring the actions and performance of health care providers – known as accreditation. Why have accreditation systems developed, what form do they take, what issues do they raise, and how useful are they in achieving the goals of health services to provide better care? To understand accreditation it is necessary to understand its history and its place in the health care environment of each country in which it operates. The information presented here is based upon the findings from a research project into the policy implications of accreditation, funded by the Department of Health and the NHS Executive. The book is divided into three parts: the first examines the history and structure of accreditation systems. Part II looks at the issues in the design and implementation of accreditation systems; and Part III addresses wider policy implications of accreditation systems.

Chapter 1 examines the idea of accreditation – what is it, why should we be interested in it? A historical description of the development of whole hospital accreditation systems in the USA, Canada and Australia is presented. The largest accreditation system in the USA, the Joint Commission on the Accreditation of Healthcare Organizations (JCAHO) can be traced back to 1917. The American College of Surgeons (ACS) was interested in creating an appropriate environment in which clinicians could practise. The hospitals took to it and by 1950 the ACS was accrediting 50 per cent of US hospitals, out of their own pockets. They could no longer afford to continue so they joined with the American College of Physicians, and other national bodies to launch the Joint Commission on Hospital Accreditation. Today the JCAHO has national coverage and is rapidly moving into the accreditation of long-term care, ambulatory care, mental health and also what they term networks, which include Health Maintenance Organizations (HMOs). The JCAHO is allowed in 42 states to replace state inspections. It has, in part, become a branch of the government regulatory processes.

The Canadian Council on Health Facilities Accreditation (CCHFA) began when Canada decided to leave membership of the JCAHO in the 1950s and formed its own national accreditation system. It subsequently developed its own structure, standards and methods of assessment. Unlike the JCAHO it had the support of the Federal Government which has maintained an arm's length relationship with it. The Canadian system now covers approximately 97 per cent of all hospital beds. The Government claims no direct interest in the results of accreditation, but depends upon it to ensure standardization of quality of service delivery across the provinces.

Australia started out trying to introduce accreditation in 1926 but only succeeded in the 1970s. It began as a state initiative and did not take off until it managed to receive national funding. The Australian Council on Healthcare Standards (ACHS) has slowly developed over time and still has some way to go to achieve national coverage. The Australian government has encouraged its development and is now considering tying bonus medicare payments to high scoring institutions.

So why did all these countries manage to go down this route, when the UK which has been talking about accreditation for a decade at least, has not managed to develop such a system?

Chapter 2 tries to answer this question. There have been many calls for accreditation in recent times. But the Royal Colleges are not interested in it, the government has set its face against it until recently (hence the research I have been asked to conduct). Instead the UK has developed a multitude of small, underdeveloped accreditation systems. The providers are demonstrating their desire for such systems. A survey of all Trust Chief Executives (response rate 70 per cent) has shown considerable support for the idea but no single view about implementation. Inevitably, the new systems which are developing are piecemeal, directed at specific services or professional departments and have little coherence. The only system which is a contender to be a national accreditation system is run by the King Edward VII Hospital Fund for London.

The NHS Executive is facing some complicated policy questions as it has to decide whether to promote accreditation. To a large extent the policy decision rests upon whether there is a strong desire by the government to control or monitor provider activity or to use accreditation as a means to standardize purchaser definitions of quality. This chapter lays out the policy questions which are facing the government of the UK (and indeed any government which is considering a system of national standards and quality control).

But of course it all depends upon what accreditation actually achieves – and whether it provides value for money. It is not the only approach to monitoring standards available to a health service.

Chapter 3 reports on the research findings from the Department of Health funded study of units which have been through either the King's Fund Organisational Audit or the Hospital Accreditation Programme developed in the South West. What does it feel like to go through accreditation? What benefit does a unit derive from the process? What are the benefits? What are the disadvantages? How does accreditation fit into a unit's management approach? Is it simply an exercise in rubber stamping, or does it have some greater value to the organization? Can it tell us how well managers or clinicians are doing or how safe a hospital is?

Chapter 4 examines the problems encountered in the setting of standards. Standards are central to any accreditation system. But they are not easy to define and set. They can be directed at whole organizations, departments, professional groups; they can be minimum, optimum, resource constrained or idealistic. How are they set? The JCAHO is constrained by the market – if a standard is not achievable it is abandoned. The CCHFA uses extensive consultation with all its participants to get agreement on standards. How should compliance with them be scored? The JCAHO has complex algorithms to determine scores (it has to as a score will determine whether a hospital gets funding); CCHFA permits more subjective surveyor judgement on five different dimensions; Australia has the most subjective system. But the scoring depends upon the model for accreditation – is it about pronouncing degrees of safety and the potential for success, or is it about education and institutional development?

Chapter 5 looks at the organizational issues facing accreditation systems and draws on a comparison of the approaches adopted by the USA, Canadian and Australian systems. Each accreditation system has a board which controls its activities. Each country has a very different board composition. All are increasing their consumer representation. Traditionally accreditation was a private activity – the results only known to the participating organization. Today the JCAHO has been forced to make its findings public – in response to consumer pressure. Canada just announces which hospitals have been through the programme. The USA system, tied as it is to government and insurance funding, is crucial to the financial health of many hospitals. There have to be appeal procedures to allow those who feel they have been treated unfairly to have the decision reviewed. The JCAHO has some full-time surveyors. Canada and ACHS use only professional practitioners borrowed to undertake the surveys. The credibility of accreditation depends upon the selection of the surveyors. ACHS has very strict rules of eligibility for surveyors. There are questions about whether surveyors should be given knowledge of previous surveys or whether they should examine each hospital on its current performance. Should surveys be planned or should they be spot checks? This chapter examines the complex issues faced by the accreditation systems in determining their internal organization.

Chapter 6 looks at the wider policy implications of accreditation. The world is changing, management theories are developing, there are growing concerns about costs, there are many more stakeholders who have an interest in the results of accreditation. Are the interests different if the funders of health care are private or public bodies? Or if the providers are privately or publicly owned? There are legal issues developing, particularly in Canada about the status of standards. An organization which participates in accreditation is deemed to have accepted the standards as minimal (as opposed to the optimal nature intended by all the accreditation programmes). Can a hospital be sued for failing to comply with standards? What does this mean for the NHS or other health systems considering accreditation? What are the options for the organization of accreditation systems?

Chapter 7 looks to the future of accreditation. The Joint Commission on Accreditation of Health Care Organizations has been developing clinical performance indicators to move its assessments from 'what could be done' to 'what is being done'. Where does that leave the future of accreditation systems? How far have they moved from their origins? Are they likely to be able to sustain themselves in the health care systems? What will their relationship with government and consumers be in the future? Where does accreditation fit in the complex notions of quality? All claim to be part of the Continuous Quality Improvement School of thought but critics argue that they are undermining the total quality management approach. Consumers want to know they are safe and protected. But is this form of external review contrary to quality as the search for excellence? Accreditation systems began as the protectors of the professionals. They are moving to providing information to consumers to make choices between health care providers. Is this the future for accreditation?

PART I

THE HISTORY AND STRUCTURE OF ACCREDITATION SYSTEMS

1

THE ESSENCE OF ACCREDITATION

The present Holy Grail of the health services world is quality – that indescribable, mystical sense of doing what you do well, of striving continuously to seek self-improvement. The talk is of quality services and quality relationships, some aimed at making patients healthier, better, happier; some aimed merely at the chance of doing what is done, somehow, better. New and different ways of conceptualizing quality, new approaches to its measurement and implementation are continuously washing through the health services. Some are based upon eternal truths, like religion, to be believed unquestioningly. Know yourself better and you will do better. Others are more mechanistic, there is a right way of doing things. Let us agree it and find ways of enacting it.

Within the quality movement there is an approach which is gaining considerable popularity. It is called accreditation. Accreditation is a system of external peer review for determining compliance with a set of standards. It is concerned with the quality of health care delivery but traditionally, its approach has been based upon the belief that hospitals should be safe places in which professionals should practise and patients should be cared for. Unlike the philosophies of quality management, it is based on a premise that there are certain actions which should be undertaken in order to be 'a good hospital', and much of the concern is with the protection of patients and staff.

Everyone who has been a patient must have experienced a concern, however small, that the people treating them might make a basic administrative error which could result in a catastrophic outcome. You might be ascribed the wrong medical record, and treated for a condition suffered by someone with a similar name. You might be given the wrong medication. In an emergency, you might be treated by equipment which does not work. Imagine collapsing in need of resuscitation, only to find that the life-saving equipment did not work. Worse than that, you might be treated by an unqualified doctor, nurse or other health professional. Worse still, you might be treated by someone who is mentally unstable, interested only in causing harm or death. All of these things have happened in the history of every health service. All are thought to be preventable if the right precautions are taken by the hospital authorities.

Patients tend to assume that hospitals, being buildings in public use, whoever owns them, are safe. Patients rarely review buildings, prior to admission, to ensure that in the event of fire, the fire escapes are clear. They do not tend to do tours of hospitals to check whether the kitchens are hygienic and the food stored properly. Yet everyone is aware of stories of salmonella outbreaks in hospitals, resulting in the death of vulnerable patients. But how can members of the public be reassured that the hospital is as safe as it should be? One answer is that the hospital should be able to demonstrate that it operates to agreed rules of behaviour, good practice which will minimize the risks attendant in running a large and extremely complex organization. No one would deny that things can go wrong in even the best run places, but it surely is expected that every member of staff will try to strive to do their best to ensure safety. After all, it is in their own best interests too.

But as the catalogue of familiar disasters outlined above shows, precautions can be overlooked. Patients can be put at risk. The only way therefore to be sure that the hospital environment is safe is to check. All governments provide for inspections to check on basic environmental safety but these will not cover all of the issues raised above. Nor will they guarantee that in the time between the inspections, standards are being maintained. The solution therefore appears to lie in the hands of the hospital managers and staff to ensure that practices are kept at the appropriate standard.

But in health care this is only half the story. Patients and local communities need to know that their health care needs are being met adequately. Traditionally this was left to the professionals to determine. Recently, there have been many arguments claiming that the key to knowing whether care is adequate lies in patient satisfaction, and there has been growing interest in the use of patient views in determining quality. But both these approaches contain flaws.

It is not sufficient to rely on the praise or criticism of patients, because their assessments are notoriously subjective and unscientific. Similarly, the medical staff of a hospital are not the best people to make an objective assessment of their own hospital. In the smaller towns the medical staff tend to be associated only with their own hospital and thus lack the background to compare their hospital's performance against that of similar institutions conducted by others. While the medical staff of a large teaching hospital may have knowledge of other hospitals, their interest is often in a rather narrow specialty and consequently they lack the knowledge to make an assessment of the total hospital performance.

(National Hospital 1969: 10)

And so standards, agreed levels of practice and conduct are required, to which all staff can work and use in their daily activities. And this is the logic of accreditation: the setting of standards which will help individuals to monitor their own behaviour and ensure that they are doing all the things expected of them. If the compliance with standards is checked by professional peers, this is the process of accreditation.

SEMANTICS AND DEFINITIONS

The language of accreditation is complicated. There are a number of words with which accreditation is frequently confused – licensure, certification, authorization, inspection and regulation (see Table 1.1). Accreditation is also used in the same breath as words such as education, consultation, participation and professionalization. Accreditation is often used to describe the process of licensing training posts, facilities or practitioners as qualified to train professional staff, particularly doctors. But this is not the activity focused on in the debate outlined here, that is, accreditation as the process of evaluating the functioning of health care organizations. It can be applied to whole hospitals, to service delivery systems (increasingly called networks in the United States) and professional activities. The earliest and most common form of accreditation concentrated on whole health service organizations – mostly hospitals.

Accreditation systems were designed originally to protect the medical profession from the worst effects of poor environments and

Table 1.1 Definitions

License	to authorize by legal grant or permission
Certificate	a written testament of ability
Authorize	to make legitimate by authority
Inspect	to view and examine officially
Regulate	to control or order by restrictions

poor organizations. This aspect of quality has been carried forward into the present quality debates of the health care professionals. It is held that all practice can be improved – thus, an integral part of professionalism is continuous striving to achieve better standards. In part this reflects improved physical environments, in part reflects new treatments and better clinical approaches. The story of accreditation shows the move from an emphasis upon environment to clinical practice. It demonstrates the role of accreditation as a tool in the wider political environment of health care systems. Accreditation systems have to reflect local political realities for them to have meaning and credence in their health care systems.

THE NATURE OF ACCREDITATION

In its pure form accreditation has a number of distinct characteristics. Participation in any accreditation scheme is voluntary. There must be standards against which the operation of the participating organization can be assessed. Compliance with the standards must be conducted by assessors who are independent of the participating organization. There must be an outcome from the accreditation in the form of a pass or fail, or a scaled grading which denotes compliance with the standards.

Accreditation is therefore an act of voluntary submission to review by external agents. In many cases the review is undertaken by peers who can assist in ensuring that the organization meets the standards of the professional group to which it belongs. Thus, it is equally an exposure to one's professional peers, providing the opportunity for peers to say whether a good job is being done and to point out areas of vulnerability to outside criticism. Accreditation by peers is a non-threatening method of gaining both recognition for good work, and help where there are deficiencies in practice.

Accreditation also contains an indicator of level of success, the accreditation status. This is considered to be an integral part of the accreditation process. To an extent, it mimics a model of professional rather than perhaps managerial assessment. Professionals are used to being harshly assessed by their educators – their training invariably concludes with the taking of examinations which a certain number are expected to fail. Professionals learn early on to operate to norms of behaviour and appreciate that some must fail for standards to be maintained. For this reason, knowledge of the grading which follows the accreditation survey was kept confidential to the participating organization. Entry for the examination and an unfortunate outcome would not be made public.

But accreditation systems have focused upon the environment in which professionals practice. And the environment has become the domain of the managers, who hold different views of the world, and operate to different norms and expectations. Their outlook encompasses wider, collective and societal concerns. Accreditation for them, should conform to a different model. It offers a means of communicating success to the outside world. And once this has occurred, a wider interest in the outcome of the accreditation process inevitably follows. The general public, funders (public or insurers), and governments all have legitimate interests in knowing how safe hospitals are. Few accreditation systems have managed to resist the demands, made by funders and public bodies in the name of accountability, for knowledge of how well an organization is doing relative to others. In giving in to these demands, the accreditation systems move from being part of a voluntary professional support system to becoming part of the wider network of activities designed to promote the public interest. And here it is possible to see why accreditation becomes confused with licensure and authorization. When state regulation – either for funding purposes or as a means of policing the public environment – begins to use accreditation to supplement its activities, the role of accreditation changes from the professional model of education and support to one of control. Standards become minimal hurdles to be crossed rather than guidelines for good practice. Surveyors change their role from educators and professional reviewers to that of inspectors. Regulations may be formulated that require an organization to achieve a certain accreditation level as a condition of licence to practise or to receive public funding.

The independent nature of the accreditation process, in its original form, also means that accreditation tends to be a private sector or non-governmental activity. Most of the accreditation systems operate as not-for-profit businesses, financing themselves by levying fees for their work. This means that they operate from the basis of either voluntary sector or private sector principles. They have to recognize the needs of their customers who pay their fees which in most cases will be the organizations being surveyed.

So, in whose interest should the accreditation bodies act? The professions whose standards they should seek to uplift and pro-mote; the organizations whose relationship with the professional bodies, at least in health care may be somewhat at odds; the regulatory bodies of governments who are supposed to act in the public interest; or the public themselves who may have some very different views of how services should behave? The history of the development of accreditation systems in the Anglophone countries shows how these questions have impinged upon the development of accreditation systems and the solutions that have been sought.

THE HISTORY OF ACCREDITATION

Hospital accreditation is a product of the Anglophone countries: the United States, Canada, and Australia. They all share a similar genesis. They are all, ultimately, derived from the American model, the pioneer of accreditation. They form, as it were, a family group. There are other approaches which are nearer other models. Catalonia developed an approach which is the product of public legislation and is therefore much nearer the regulatory model. The same is true of China. But the Anglophone model has captured the world's imagination and is being copied across the globe, in the United Kingdom, South Africa, New Zealand and Holland to name but a few.

A study of the background of accreditation systems reveals the inextricable link between accreditation and the structure and funding mechanisms of the health service to which it is applied. Accreditation, it transpires, is a process with many uses, social, economic and inevitably, political. Each country has developed its own approach to the structure of the accreditation body, its functioning, and its application to the delivery of health care.

THE UNITED STATES

Accreditation in the United States is the product of an initiative taken by the medical profession. In 1910, Dr Ernest Codman developed what he called the 'end-result system' of hospital organization (Roberts *et al.* 1987). The system purported to enable a hospital to track every patient it treated, with the main purpose of establishing whether the treatment was effective. This system had a great appeal at the time, when hospital standards were known to vary widely. It would enable the standardization of hospitals 'on the basis of service to the individual patient, as demonstrated by available records' (Roberts *et al.* 1987). The end result was the founding of the American College of Surgeons in 1913, which was firmly espoused to the concept of hospital standardization.

In 1917 the American College of Surgeons established the Hospital Standardization Programme. The aim of this was, in the words of its main architect, to ensure

> that those institutions having the highest ideals may have proper recognition before the profession, and that those of inferior equipment and standards should be stimulated to raise the quality of their work. In this way patients will receive the best type of treatment, and the public will have some means of recognizing those institutions devoted to the highest ideals of medicine.
>
> (Roberts *et al.* 1987: 936)

One of the earliest requirements for membership of the American College of Surgeons was the production of case records as evidence of surgical skill. It was found to be difficult to implement as many hospitals did not keep adequate records. With support from the American Hospital Association and the Catholic Hospital Conference, an investigation into hospitals in the USA and Canada showed the absence of any records in many hospitals. The results were so poor that after their presentation at a conference in the Waldorf-Astoria Hotel in New York the report was burnt in the hotel's furnaces.

The accreditation initiative was part of the wider transformation in American medicine at the time (Rosenberg 1987; Starr 1982): the celebration of medicine seen as science, of which the Flexner report was perhaps the most important symbol. Hospitals, from treating primarily the indigent and the chronically ill, became the laboratory for producing health. As such they began to attract paying patients and to become increasingly dependent on the income thus generated. In turn, this meant that the hospitals became dependent on the attendant physicians who brought in the paying patients. The rise of scientific medicine thus brought about a change in the

Table 1.2   The ACAS minimum standard

---

1 That physicians and surgeons privileged to practise in the hospital be
organized as a definite group or staff. Such organization has nothing to
do with the question as to whether the hospital is 'open' or 'closed', nor
need it affect the various existing types of staff organization. The word
STAFF here is defined as the group of doctors who practise in the
hospital inclusive of all groups such as the 'regular staff', the 'visiting
staff', and the 'associate staff'.

2 That membership upon the staff be restricted to physicians and
surgeons who are (a) full graduates of medicine in good standing and
legally licensed to practise in their respective states or provinces, (b)
competent in their respective fields, (c) worthy in character and in
matters of professional ethics; that in this latter connection the practice
of the division of fees, under any guise whatever, be prohibited.

3 That the staff initiate and, with the approval of the governing body of
the hospital, adopt rules, regulations and policies governing the
professional work of the hospital; that these rules, regulations and
policies specifically provide: (a) that staff meetings be held at least once
a month, (b) that the staff review and analyse at regular intervals their
clinical experience in the various departments of the hospital, such as
medicine, surgery, obstetrics, and the other specialties; the clinical
records of patients, free and pay, to be the basis for such review and
analyses.

4 That accurate and complete records be written for all patients and filed
in an accessible manner in the hospital – a complete case record being
one which includes identification data; complaint, personal and family
history; history of present illness; physical examination; special
examinations such as consultations, clinical laboratory, X-ray and other
examinations; provisional or working diagnosis; medical or surgical
treatment; gross and microscopical pathological examinations; progress
notes, final diagnosis; condition on discharge; follow-up and, in case of
death, autopsy findings.

5 That diagnostic and therapeutic facilities under competent supervision
be available for the study, diagnosis and treatment of patients, these to
include, at least (a) a clinical laboratory providing chemical,
bacteriological, serological, and pathological services; (b) an X-ray
department providing radiographic and fluoroscopic services.

Source: ACS Bulletin, 24

balance of power between the medical profession – which, in effect,
controlled the market for patients – and the hospital administration.

The Hospital Standardization Programme, as originally con-
ceived, was one of the means by which the American medical elite

asserted its claim to control the system in which its members worked. It may well have had other purposes. But, if we examine the five standards initially laid down (see Table 1.2), it is clear that the programme represented an assertion of medical autonomy as against the Trustees and administrators who had traditionally dominated the hospital scene.

The standards were very obviously directed at creating an adequate environment in which doctors could practise their craft. Three of the standards were concerned with the organization of the medical staff: the aim was to ensure that the medical staff should collectively determine the rules, regulations and policies affecting the 'professional work of the hospital' and that they should have the power to exclude those physicians who were not considered to be adequately qualified or competent. The fourth standard dealt with medical records, while the fifth sought to ensure that the technical resources required for the practice of scientific medicine – that is, the appropriate diagnostic and therapeutic facilities – were available.

The College surveyors originally had 18 pages of text to follow which contained the standard, a statement on the application of principles and an explanation and extension of each principle. Additionally, there was a statement on the 'By-products of Standardization' which was based on 13,360 surveys over the preceding nine years. This pointed to the need for 'more attention focused on the patient, better organization, personnel, facilities, and procedures; better cooperation and coordination; and improved end results in patient care' (Stephenson 1981). And this has been the driving aim of hospital accreditation throughout its development.

Over time, the number of standards multiplied, as did the number of hospitals submitting themselves to the accreditation process. By 1949 over half the hospitals in the United States were involved and the standardization manuals increased to 118 pages. A method of evaluation had been introduced known as the Points Rating System. To attain a perfect score, a hospital had to achieve 640 essential points and 260 complementary points. At this time it was felt the programme became too expensive for the College of Surgeons to carry on its own. By 1950 it had cost over $2 million, the whole cost borne by the College from its membership fees. The American College of Surgeons approached the College of Physicians and the American Hospitals Association and other bodies to join with them to create the Joint Commission on Accreditation of Hospitals (re-named in 1988 the Joint Commission on Accreditation of Healthcare Organizations (JCAHO)).

As before, the medical profession dominated the organization, although the American Hospital Association also secured representation. Until 1993, the 24-strong Board of Commissioners was composed of members nominated by the American Medical Association, the American College of Surgeons, the American Dental Association, the American Hospitals Association and one consumer representative. In 1993 the JCAHO added four more seats to its member board, three public and one nursing.

The accreditation system evolved a set of scores to signal how well a hospital complied with standards. By the early 1990s this had become a four staged outcome measure of the level of compliance with the standards: accreditation with commendation (which covers only about 5 per cent of the hospitals surveyed); accreditation with no recommendations; accreditation with recommendations; and lastly conditional accreditation for cases where there are major deficiencies and the organization is given six months in which to make sufficient progress to move into one of the other categories. The surveyors too had changed – they are now taken from a pool of practising health professionals, retired health professionals and a small number of full-time employees.

In essence, the accreditation system developed by the JCAHO would therefore appear to be a model of self-regulation by the health care industry. However, just as the original initiative was driven in part at least by changes in the medical marketplace, so the JCAHO has been forced to adapt to the changes brought about in the 1960s by the introduction of Medicare and Medicaid. This, in effect, made hospitals dependent on revenue from tax-financed patients. Public finance brought about a threat of public regulation: the reimbursement of Medicare patients was made dependent on hospitals meeting the federal conditions, enforced by the states, for participation. In effect the state was determining hospital standards. If the JCAHO was to head off the threat of a federal inspectorate – and with it, a threat to its own survival – it had to adapt. A compromise was negotiated. Hospitals accredited by the JCAHO were given 'deemed status', that is, they were deemed to have met the conditions necessary for participation in Medicare. At present 42 states allow hospitals exemption from their own regulatory processes if they have received the imprimatur of the JCAHO. Of the approximately 7,000 hospitals meeting the conditions for deemed status for Medicare, about 77 per cent do so through the JCAHO accreditation programme.

In principle, then, the twin-defining characteristics of an

accreditation system – contrasted with a system of state regulation – have been maintained. The body defining and monitoring standards in the United States remains independent: participation in the scheme is voluntary. In practice, both principles have been blurred. In a sense, the JCAHO is both competing with the federal government and dependent on it when it comes to writing standards: it has become, as it were, part of the public system. Many of its standards were used in devising the federal and state regulations; conversely, however, some of its standards, notably those dealing with fire safety, have been tightened up in response to pressure from the federal bureaucracy (Legge 1982). Significantly too, its 1970 accreditation manual signalled a move from minimum to optimum achievable standards. And to some extent the drift away from protecting the public from poor hospital care to professionalizing the quality of care began. The change heralded the birth of the quality movement in health care. The emphasis shifted from protecting the doctor and the patient from poor administration to a different perception, in which health care was analysed from a systems point of view and quality became viewed as a function of the processes of care.

Although hospitals are not compelled to seek JCAHO accreditation, they have a very strong incentive to do so – and 80 per cent participate (the main exceptions being small rural hospitals). Although the JCAHO does not have a monopoly – there are a number of other accreditation programmes in the United States – it remains the dominant player in the field.

In many ways, the JCAHO's evolving strategy during the 1980s can be understood as the response of any large institution – which is precisely what it has become – to challenges or threats in its market position in a changing environment. In the USA not only is changing professional opinion reforming the philosophy of accreditation, but market forces are also at work. The JCAHO has been in a position of near monopoly for many years. However, as it has extended its reach into other areas such as home care it has begun to face competition which is causing it to change the basis of its accreditation approach. The Professional Standards Review Organizations were introduced to enhance the quality assurance in hospitals through the voluntary review of professional standards and thus came into direct competition with the then Joint Commission on Accreditation of Hospitals in terms of medical quality assurance (Palmer 1978). The Community Health Accreditation Program (CHAP), developed by the National League for Nursing, to deal with community services, operates under a different philosophy. Whereas the JCAHO has three-yearly, pre-planned visits and discloses its findings only to the hospital surveyed, the Community Health Accreditation has annual unannounced visits and provides for disclosure of information on its findings. Two organizations which have supported the CHAP in preference to the JCAHO, the National Consumers' League and the People's Medical Society, charged that the JCAHO has an unfair marketing advantage through its practices. In response the JCAHO agreed to move to some (5 per cent) annual visits without advance notice and to submit its accreditation findings to Health Care Financing Administration (American Journal of Nursing 1992). It continues to offer organizations not interested in deemed status the option of staying on the three-year accreditation cycle. As the external agencies are demanding a different approach the JCAHO is forced to respond to meet their needs. In addition it has extended its scope: it has widened its accreditation activities not only to cover long-term care, ambulatory facilities and home care (Roberts *et al.* 1987), but also agencies which coordinate care, referred to as networks. A health care network is an entity that directly provides, or provides for integrated health services to a defined population. A network may offer comprehensive or specialty services. It must have a central structure which coordinates service delivery. The types of organization covered by the definition of a network are HMOs, preferred provider organizations, physicians and hospital organizations, and specialty networks which offer services to HMOs – for example, mental health services, and government systems which cover for example Veterans.

In 1985, the JCAHO initiated a radical change in direction, to respond to changes in perceptions within the health care field relating to quality, and to reposition itself in the marketplace. Analysis of survey results had shown that organizations in general, and clinicians in particular, were not sufficiently interested in the quality of care evaluations. This resulted in a three pronged approach to quality, published in 1987 as a development programme entitled 'The Agenda for Change'. First, the JCAHO decided to move to a more clinical emphasis in its monitoring activities, through the development of severity adjusted clinical performance measures (a move on the way to outcome measures). Second, it revisited its whole approach to assessing organizational performance. Third, it launched a new approach to diversify and expand its educational role, to move it away from the purely monitoring role (O'Leary 1991). The details of these approaches will be reviewed in later chapters.

CANADA

The Canadian Council on Hospital Accreditation (rechristened the Canadian Council on Health Facilities Accreditation in 1988) was set up in 1953, following several years of preparation. It was a breakaway from the JCAHO: a Canadian declaration of independence to meet the needs of the newly established Canadian National Health System. The initiative came from the medical profession and the hospitals' association. The Canadian Medical Association set up a committee to investigate the possibility of a Canadian Accreditation programme. In 1952, the Canadian Medical Association met with representatives of the Canadian Hospitals Association, the Royal College of Physicians and Surgeons and L'Association des médicins de langue français du Canada and together they established the Canadian Commission on Hospital Accreditation. It was felt that 'the national status of Canada, its language and racial factors and its changing economies in the hospital service, called for the establishment of a purely Canadian program for hospital accreditation' (Canadian Council on Health Facilities Accreditation 1992).

Like the JCAHO, it is an autonomous independent body. But unlike the JCAHO, it received its official recognition early in its existence, receiving its Letter Patent from the Secretary of State in 1958. As such, it is the sole authority to accredit hospitals in Canada: that is, it has the monopoly of accreditation activities which now encompass long-term, mental health and rehabilitation facilities as well as general hospitals. It has an arm's length relationship with government, with government observers on its board, but no formal relationship.

As in the case of the JCAHO, the CCHFA's history is one of steady expansion through its history: by the end of the 1980s, it was accrediting something like 1,300 facilities (over 94 per cent of hospital beds). Again, it has moved from minimum to optimum achievable standards, by which is meant 'the best possible level that can be achieved given the available resources' (Canadian Council on Health Facilities Accreditation: 8 1992). Like the JCAHO, it grades the results of its accreditation visits: the range is from

non-accreditation to a four-year accreditation, with four inter-
mediate awards. Finally, it engages in a continual process of
revising its standards: a process which culminated in a major
consultation exercise that led to the publication of a shorter,
revised standards document in 1990.

In all these respects, the CCHFA has moved in parallel with the
JCAHO. Interestingly, though, it has done so without the goad of
changes in public policy. There is nothing in Canada equivalent to
the Medicare requirement for meeting standards as a condition for
getting reimbursements. The client for accreditation reviews in
Canada is still very much the individual hospital: the accreditation
process, in the words of the CCHFA, 'acts as a yardstick by which
health care organizations can measure their own performance
against national standards'. Its function is to identify opportunities
for improvement and to educate staff (Canadian Council on
Health Facilities Accreditation 1992). But accreditation has
moved towards regulation, at least for training purposes, in that it
is a requirement for hospitals wishing to train medical interns and
other health professionals. In addition, there is some evidence that
the funders – that is, the provincial governments – are beginning to
take an interest in accreditation reports.

But the Canadian system has evolved differently from the
American model in some important respects. It is much less
bureaucratic and legalistic. Before 1970, one surveyor was assigned to a hospital for one day. In 1970 they moved to team
surveys with doctors and nurses. In the mid-1970s, the team size
increased to the now familiar three including a hospital adminis-
trator. All surveyors are practitioners working within the health
care system. The composition of its 14-member board is significantly different: the nominees of the medical profession account
for less than half the membership and two are nominated by the
Canadian Nurses Association. The accreditation documentation is
much less complex. There is much less emphasis on trying to
reduce the discretion of surveyors by elaborate scoring systems.
Canada's experience has been similar to that of the USA, different
in that it operates in a different health care environment and does
not face the competitive threats of other accreditation systems.
But it too has reviewed its standards, widened its scope, and
reconstituted its board and continued to work to maintain its
relevance to the health care environment. It, too, has been
extending its coverage to other areas of the health care sector and
has moved in the direction of new standards which cut across

existing hospital departmental boundaries to review the experience of patients as they move through the health care system.

AUSTRALIA

An interest in hospital accreditation first appeared in Australia in 1926. The governments of New South Wales, Victoria and New Zealand agreed to a request from the then Australian Branch of the British Medical Association to finance a study into the feasibility of introducing the USA system into Australia and New Zealand. The Director of the American College of Surgeons' Hospital standardization programme was invited to conduct the study. He did not specifically recommend the introduction of a hospital standardization programme and in consequence interest waned until the 1950s (Duckett 1983). In 1946 the Australian Hospitals' Association (AHA) was established with terms of reference which included 'to co-operate in ensuring higher standards, greater efficiency and improved conditions for patients'. The AHA then began to move towards the idea of accreditation and invited the Royal Australasian College of Physicians and the College of Surgeons to join with them. The Royal Australasian College of Surgeons agreed to cooperate in developing standards but would not accept representation on any assessment body. Unlike the USA, interest from the surgeons was therefore limited.

Two hospitals volunteered to be reviewed against the USA standards in 1950. After this initial pilot, other hospitals were invited to volunteer – but none did. It was only in 1959, that the Australian Medical Association's New South Wales Branch decided to promote the idea of accreditation and created a committee with representatives from the RACS, the RACP and College of General Practitioners and the Postgraduate Committee in Medicine in the University of Sydney. In 1960, an accreditation system using standards from the USA was established in New South Wales. But it was not supported by the Hospitals Commission of New South Wales. Furthermore, the organization of the public hospital services was being examined by a Ministerial Committee. It in turn recommended that standards should be a statutory responsibility rather than an independent one, and the accreditation committee was abandoned. The State of Victoria was also becoming interested in the idea of accreditation and a similar accreditation committee, established in Victoria, agreed to pilot the standards developed in New South Wales. The Victoria branch of the AHA was promoting the idea of a national accreditation system. In 1968 a joint committee of the two associations was established to explore ways of introducing accreditation. The Kellogg Foundation and the Royal Clinical Colleges were also approached for funding but this was unsuccessful. In 1971 the joint committee approached the Director General of Health to ask for federal government support. At this meeting it was pointed out that the Canadian government had helped establish their accreditation system, so why couldn't the Australian government offer equivalent help?

In 1973 the joint committee approached the federal government for funding and received grants to appoint a full-time director. The first director had had considerable experience in Canada. Victoria agreed to participate in some pilot surveys but New South Wales announced it was considering setting up its own system. In 1974 the committee was relaunched as The Australian Council on Hospitals Standards (subsequently renamed the Australian Council on Healthcare Standards). There then followed intensive debates with governmental bodies about the appropriate composition and terms of reference of the accrediting body. Finally, in 1977 the full membership of the Australian Council on Healthcare standards was agreed. Its tentative beginnings in Victoria, developed into New South Wales, later extending to other states: the Australian Capital Territory and Northern Territory in 1979 and South Australia in 1980 (Duckett and Coombs 1981).

The Australian experience is different from that of the USA and Canada. Although there had been a recognition of accreditation since the 1920s, the surgeons were reluctant to be involved. However, the American Medical Association (AMA) saw the introduction of a voluntary scheme of self-regulation, under its control, as a way of heading off the possibility of a system of government regulation. The AHA hoped that independently set standards would force the government to inject the resources required to achieve them – in other words, accreditation was perceived to be a way of bringing pressure on funders. In addition, hospital administrators appear to have seen accreditation as an instrument for controlling medical staff.

The accreditation programme was designed 'to assure interested groups that the health professionals consider it a responsibility to monitor the standards of performance of their members' and in addition, 'the Council must emphasize both utilization of resources and the quality of care provided by those resources' (Australian Council on Hospital Standards (1978: xii)).

The ACHS system has a number of different accreditation decisions: full accreditation which is three years, partial accreditation of one year or no accreditation. A new five-year level of accreditation status is about to be introduced, should an organization be awarded three years' accreditation in three consecutive years.

In the outcome, the ACHS emerged as an independent body, very much on the North American Model. As in the United States, the medical profession has a majority of the membership of the 22 member board, although nurses, allied health professionals and consumers are also represented, albeit sparsely. From the start, it stressed that its role is 'evaluative and educative rather than inspectorial or judgemental' (McCue and Wilson 1981). As in the case of Canada, inspections are carried out by doctors, nurses and administrators who are seconded for the task. As in the case of Canada, the bureaucratic complexities of the JCAHO model appear to have been avoided. Its major impact has been felt in the private sector rather than the public although it is beginning to develop a close relationship with a number of state governments.

Like its North American counterparts, the ACHS has adapted its system over the years. The ACHS puts much emphasis on reviewing the quality assurance activities of the facilities being accredited, as part of its emphasis on promoting 'continuing improvement in the quality of care delivered', in the words of the 1993 Accreditation Guide (The Australian Council on Healthcare Standards 1993). The intent is that the facility must demonstrate that it is 'conducting its own ongoing evaluation of outcome, for the purpose of identifying areas of concern and effecting necessary changes to continually improve the standards of care provided.'

The Australian system is still developing. The system has not yet achieved the extensive coverage in terms of numbers of hospital beds of the other countries' systems. The highest coverage achieved by 1994 was in Victoria, which achieved 60 per cent of beds (*The Accreditor* 1993). Following the USA model, the ACHS, in cooperation with the medical colleges, has developed a set of clinical outcome indicators, the first of which were used in accreditation reviews during 1993.

THE SIMILARITIES AND THE DIFFERENCES

All three accreditation systems have adapted their standards and their approach to assessing compliance over the years. In the late

1980s all began to consider ways of revising standards to make them more patient focused rather than professionally focused. In the 1990s they have revised their standards to reflect the changing functions of hospitals, seeking to move away from a focus on departments towards one of patient experience of hospital systems. They have all moved towards trying to find standards which would reflect the integration of hospital services rather than examining them in isolation. And finally, they have all begun to look at outcome measures instead of simple process standards for good practice.

The three accreditation systems have revised – and continue to do so – their approach to the definition and monitoring of standards in response to what might be called the 'quality movement' both within and outside health care. As Chapter 4 will show in more detail, the notion of standards implies fixed points in the definition of quality: points which may, from time to time, be ratcheted upwards, but which nevertheless provided clear cut criteria. And as the following chapters will show, the notion of quality can also imply a continual process of self-examination, a never-ending search for improvement without a fixed destination. There is a tension between these two concepts. If setting standards is seen as an exercise in public accountability (to patients and taxpayers) which at the most basic level means protection from poor management or better, the achievement of a particular level of care, it is incompatible with a concept of quality as something in a continual state of evolution. The former, however formulated, requires certainty; the latter implies continual revision.

The evolution of the JCAHO's standards can be seen as an attempt to reconcile the tension between these two concepts: in a sense it has always defined its role as being both to monitor standards and to promote self-education. Up to the mid-1980s or so, its efforts took the form of defining standards – and the criteria to be used in assessing them – ever more precisely and in greater detail. The result is a proliferation of standards – some 2,200 in all – and ever-increasing complexity in the process of scoring and assessing them in an attempt to increase objectivity. Canada has evolved an increasingly complex scoring system which is not based upon complex algorithms to calculate the final score, but based upon a multi-dimensional model which attempts to capture different aspects of service delivery. The Australian approach has remained relatively simple, asking for yes or no compliance with individual standards with criteria against which surveyors can judge compliance.

All three Anglophone systems have experienced considerable success in developing the self-regulation of the health care market. They have all achieved a near-monopoly position facing little in the way of direct competition. The JCAHO had the advantage of being first, growing rapidly and thereby prevented the development of any significant competition. Canada and Australia built upon the experience of the JCAHO and therefore were able to import a fully fledged system. All have the support of their professional medical bodies which has provided them with a significant place in the political arena of their health care systems.

Nevertheless, they have achieved this position in very different circumstances. Their experience of government support has been very different. The JCAHO pre-dated any of the present state regulatory bodies and over time these two very different approaches, peer review and state inspection, have had to learn to coexist. This remove from government is shown by the fact that there is no governmental representation on the Board of the JCAHO. The establishment of the CCHFA was supported by the government of the time and non-voting observers, representing the provinces and the federal government, attend the board meetings. The relationship is distant but mutually supportive. The CCHFA monitors the quality of Canadian hospital provision which enables the government to know what is happening without direct involvement in the process. Completely different, the ACHS has direct government membership of its board (Lewis 1984) and receives funds from the government to continue its work.

Although the approach to accreditation is basically the same in all three countries, the relationships with governments, with state regulation and funding and ultimately with the health services are very different. Accreditation must therefore be viewed within the social, economic and political context of the health services within which it operates.

The United Kingdom, in contrast, has not evolved a national accreditation system. But why, given many of the similar concerns experienced in a delivery of health care between the UK and the other Anglophone countries, has the UK turned its face against this model of national standards? The next chapter seeks to examine the issues which have prevented the development of accreditation and the likely future for it in the UK.

2

THE UNITED KINGDOM EXPERIENCE

The UK National Health Service (NHS) has shied away from the idea of any comprehensive monitoring systems although the suggestion has been made repeatedly, the first being a proposal made in 1944 by the Minister of Health to develop a hospital inspectorate. The Royal Commission (1979) proposed an independent special monitoring health authority. Similarly, the DHSS publication, *Patients First*, also suggested that groups independent of health authorities might monitor the quality of health services management (DHSS 1979). During the 1980s there were a series of initiatives designed to develop monitoring agencies (DHSS 1981). But nothing has been forthcoming. Shaw's criticism of the health service in the 1980s is as true a decade later.

> With the exception of the National Development Team and the Health Advisory service in relation to long term care, there is no comprehensive mechanism for regular review of the NHS. Instead, various groups monitor different aspects, for different reasons, using different yardsticks – and with minimal effect on the coherent functioning of the Service. Ideally a balanced review would be inherent in the process of management; but planning and evaluation have become preoccupied with resources and quantity rather than with outputs and quality.
>
> (Shaw 1982: 217–18)

Accreditation has been on the NHS agenda for a decade. In the early 1980s, Maxwell and his colleagues suggested that the JCAHO approach would be relevant for the NHS (Maxwell *et al.* 1983). Support for an accreditation agency, along the lines of the other Anglophone models was provided in the late 1980s by the National Association of Health Authorities, the Institute of Health Service

Management, and the Royal College of Nursing. The House of Commons Social Services Select Committee also called for a national quality assurance inspectorate. But even so, there has been no national response to such calls for national bodies to set and monitor standards. The result is an uneven distribution of attempts to devise and measure standards.

> Guidelines and standards have been formulated in a number of fields in the UK but their development has been uneven. There is no organisation which has responsibility for standard setting across the board and the existence of standards in any particular field therefore depends on the interests and inclinations of the bodies active in that field.
>
> (Ham and Hunter 1988: 5)

In general the NHS has had little experience of external quality review processes. There is considerable experience of regulation (in the strict sense) of the private sector of health care: independent hospitals and nursing homes have to be registered with, and inspected by, the health authorities, each of whom enjoys considerable discretion on how to interpret national guidelines. This system pre-dates the creation of the National Health Service (NHS) and has only focused on the private sector. The only example of third party independent assessment of health services is the Hospital Advisory Service (HAS) in 1969 (Klein and Hall 1974). Its remit, however, was limited to the long-stay sector of care in the NHS and, although an embryo inspectorate, it always stressed that its role was primarily to promote good practice. It never developed an explicit set of standards. The general assumption, until recently, seems to have been that the NHS's system of hierarchic control over the nation's hospitals made concern about quality and standards redundant (Day and Klein 1987a).

Since 1990, the NHS has undergone some profound changes, the most notable is the move towards what is termed the purchaser-provider split which was intended to break the traditional hierarchical management structure. District health authorities have been given budgets to spend on the health of the populations which live within their boundaries. They contract with health care providers, hospitals and community services to ensure that the health care needs of the populations are met. They can contract with both public and private providers of health care and within this framework their purchasing activities are supervised by Regional Offices.

Primary health care under the auspices of general practice is funded independently through bodies called Family Health Service Authorities. General practitioners have been given the opportunity to become purchasers of secondary care, as well as providers of primary care. These GP fundholders can purchase limited hospital services for their patients from almost any provider of their choice. The fundholders compete with the health authorities to purchase care. Hospitals and other NHS providers of services have been encouraged to become independent actors, called Trusts. Now most health care is provided by Trusts and their work is monitored by bodies working to the central NHS Executive.

The changes in approaches to quality that have taken place in the past few years began before this system of hierarchic control broke down but have been greatly accelerated as a result (Challis *et al.* 1994). There is now no line of managerial accountability that runs up and down the NHS. The new instrument of accountability is the contract (Challis *et al.* 1994). The contract enables the specification of service design, quantity and frequently includes quality. However, there are problems for both purchasers and providers when the only agreement on definition of quality can be found within the contract. The nature of quality, it transpires, is multidimensional. It can be attributed to physical environment, to service organization and to clinical treatment. Contracts are a blunt instrument to attack these many dimensions simultaneously. Contract writing has foundered as their authors have tried to cover all of these dimensions in terms of service specification. A service which transcends organizational boundaries requires contracts to be agreed with a number of different provider organizations. This difficulty is compounded when quality is added into contracts. The quality of the physical environment, or certain dimensions of service such as waiting times may be better negotiated within the framework of a whole hospital or service delivery arena, than through contracts with individual service departments. In many cases, one set of standards which guarantees a certain understood level of quality of organizational process and procedure would free up both purchaser and provider resources to concentrate on other aspects of quality within the contract.

The lack of a single national system, developed over the life of the NHS, unlike the situation in the USA or Canada, has resulted in an incoherent complex array of accreditation systems. These suggest a desperate striving for a system approximating to accreditation on the part of service providers. They are appearing in every possible part of the health service covering hospitals, both acute and community, services which span secondary and primary care and professional practices. Fully fledged accreditation systems include the King's Fund Organisational Audit (covering hospitals, primary care, community hospitals), the Hospital Accreditation Programme, Pathology, Trent Community Hospital, South Western Health Records. Struggling to find an approach to accreditation are: the speech therapists, radiologists, specialists in head injuries, nursing (national and South East Thames), South East Thames Regional System, South Western Regional System, child health computing, estates, and a number of local systems run by purchasers. In addition, the growing interest to adopt accreditation systems has caused the NHS to borrow assessment approaches from the private sector. An accreditation system designed to promote staff training and development, known as Investors in People, promoted by the Department of Trade and Industry, has become very popular. Others, based upon the Department of Health's standards for patient services, known as the Patient's Charter also took off. And a number of purchasers also began to develop assessment systems, based on standards which were referred to as accreditation systems. Many of these have been supported by the Regional Health Authorities in an attempt to encourage monitoring processes.

However, the basis appears to be moving from managerial/organizational to professionally based systems. Nursing in particular perceived accreditation as a means to develop standards after a set of serious and damaging events in which patients were murdered or damaged by a lack of appropriate professional controls on the activities of individual nurses. Accreditation is an approach which appeals to nursing. Nursing has always espoused standards as a means of controlling their activities. Evidence from Australia has shown that nursing in the early stages of the accreditation process, demonstrated the greatest response to the ACHS accreditation programme because of their relatively weak position with regard to the medical profession (Duckett and Coombs 1981). The accreditation programme provided the opportunity for nursing to begin more systematic analysis of its activities and conditions and to assert its position within the health services. The authors attribute this interest in systematic assessment to the poor status of nursing relative to the medical profession.

The resulting web of accreditation systems moved accreditation away from a single system concentrating on the whole hospital towards a complex pattern of accreditation systems, each reflecting the views and interpretations of different professional or service groups. And, as might be expected, each of these accreditation systems has a slightly different approach to implementation which demonstrates further the options available to those wishing to construct accreditation standards or systems.

The King Edward VII's Hospital Fund for London, popularly referred to as the King's Fund (see Chapter 3) evolved an accreditation system known as organizational audit, reflecting the origins of whole hospital accreditation. Based on the Australian approach to accreditation, Organisational Audit was launched to promote organizational development and education. It adopted all the elements of accreditation without the pass, fail or gradings. Its surveyors are NHS practitioners, its standards have been adapted from the Australian manual and it has developed a new variant on the accreditation process: a survey manager liaises with the participating organization to help them prepare for the survey. In the former South Western Region, a pilot scheme on accreditation of community hospitals (see Chapter 3) adapted the Canadian system and demonstrated that a fully fledged accreditation system could be used within the NHS. Its mission was more tied to ensuring the safety of local hospitals and the better use of their resources for their patients.

The other accreditation systems are run by a variety of different organizations, some part of the providing services, some from professional bodies, some from outside, some from purchasers. In some cases the standards have evolved over long periods of time, in others they have been borrowed from other systems, frequently from other countries. There are different degrees of acceptability of standards depending upon the orientation of the group which has decided to establish them. One scheme run from Trent Regional Health Authority has developed to serve community hospitals. The Trent scheme borrowed its standards and structure from the Hospital Accreditation Programme, but has developed its own variation. Unusually, the board interviews the participating organization's manager and the surveyors before determining the final grading.

The emphasis of health care is shifting away from traditional organizational based models of care towards patient care and service delivery. One scheme, developed under the auspices of South East Thames Regional Health Authority (lately South Thames) is an attempt to establish an accreditation system without reference to departmental divisions. Standards have been developed for a range of services which cut across traditional organizational boundaries. It offers a peculiar twist in the development of accreditation systems. The standards are devised by purchasers and providers together although the standards are oriented only towards provider activities.

The appetite for accreditation is not confined to provider organizations. A number of purchasers are coming together with the King's Fund to develop a system of peer review. Purchasers are being invited to review each other's work and to make recommendations for good practice.

Accreditation applied to the provision of professional services presents a number of problems and is causing a variant on the accreditation theme. First, the professionals have, as demonstrated in all health care systems, a belief that they should be represented on any body which would assess organizational standards which affect their work. For this reason, all the accreditation bodies have attempted to involve the professional colleges. Second, where assessment might look at professional practice, the United Kingdom professionals have held firm to the belief that only professionals can assess the appropriateness of professional decisions. For this reason, when accreditation appears attractive, the professionals are displaying a predisposition to develop their own systems.

Indeed, the only other fully developed accreditation scheme in the UK is run by pathology laboratory specialists. Accreditation has been offered since spring 1992 to NHS and private clinical laboratories. Like all accreditation systems it has a board, made up of people from professional bodies with NHS management representatives and other observers. The surveying team is usually two people, one consultant pathologist and one senior Medical and Laboratory Scientific Officer (MLSO). The pathology system may provide an explanation of why one scheme tends to dominate any health service system. It covers over 60 per cent of the population of pathology laboratories; public and private. Those who do not participate are the exception rather than the rule. At this point of coverage, the pathologists can question the lack of interest of those who do not participate and place concerns in the minds of purchasers about the quality of non-participants. It is possible to hypothesize that in the accreditation market, once a certain coverage is achieved, participation becomes the norm and non-participation has to be justified.

Other professional groups are beginning to express an interest in developing a similar approach. The Royal College of Radiologists (both radiologists and oncologists) have developed standards, and are looking at ways of developing their own system of assessing compliance. The British Society of Chiropodists and Podiatrists have been working on a system of independent clinical peer review. This is an accreditation process developed for one purchasing health authority. It is an example of accreditation evolving as a response to the pressures of the internal NHS market. This was developed because it was felt that

> the encouragement of plural provision of services may intro-
> duce new levels of clinical standards. In many cases these will
> be similar to those present, and competition will aim to raise
> standards overall. There is an ever present risk that unaccept-
> able standards may be introduced, and may go un-noticed until
> a crisis occurs.
> (Barking and Havering Health Authority 1993 Internal
> Memorandum)

The purchasing district health authority, wanted to be able to compare the work of private sector chiropodists with those employed by the health service, but faced the problem of not being able to assess the quality of clinical work provided by the professionals (a point we will return to in later discussion). To assure the purchaser that clinical standards were being maintained to the Society of Chiropodists' requirements, the purchaser arranged for an independent opinion on a randomly selected group of cases from each provider. This would entail the providers keeping records in a standard format. The purchaser randomly selects the cases. The details are then sent to an assessor for review. This would be followed by a visit of a trained independent assessor to the patients to review the evidence of clinical practice. As a consequence, chiropody providers wishing to tender for a contract require a certificate of practice accreditation from the Society of Chiropodists. The professional groups, although interested in accreditation are rejecting the concept of whole hospital accreditation as practised by the JCAHO or the CCHFA. Instead they are promoting professionally based accreditation, mostly on the grounds that only professionals can judge the activities of professionals. And this has a number of effects. First, it strengthens professional introspection and does little to promote the open discussion of standards. Second, it turns away from the notion that a whole organization provides a service to patients, and concentrates only upon departments and clinical areas. So, although accreditation as a process is accepted, the underlying assumptions about total service care which the USA, Canadian and Australian systems have been trying to promote are lost.

As Chapter 3 will show in more detail, part of this divide and conquer mentality stems from a lack of universal agreement on the type of standards which should be developed. One Regional Health Authority (formerly South Western) has attempted to develop an accreditation system for nursing services based on standards which reflect performance evaluation rather than the traditional predetermined standards which concentrate on structures and processes. This is, as later chapters will show, the trend which is being set by the JCAHO in its 'Agenda for Change'. 'The performance evaluation model is based within the concept of continuous quality improvement and requires the measurement of performance through the use of reliable statistical methods and the use of information to review and modify practice.' (South Western Regional Health Authority 1993). This newly developing accreditation system has rejected the evolutionary process of accreditation through organizational standards to clinical performance measures, preferring to launch straight into the second stage. The system is designed so that provider units will provide evidence of achievement comprising relevant output/outcome trend data demonstrating effective change and commitment to quality improvement.

Medical records have always been a significant part of any of the organizationally based accreditation systems. It is therefore, perhaps, not surprising that this has been considered a suitable activity for accreditation. A very well developed system, based in the South West exists. It has standards for the management of medical records (see Table 2.1). There are nine standards, each of which is accompanied by criteria to assess compliance with the standard. Participating hospitals complete a self-assessment questionnaire based on the published standards. A team of at least two surveyors (from different parts of the region) visits the site to discuss and observe the application of the standards. After a final discussion with local managers the surveyors prepare a written report detailing comments, commendations and recommendations. There is a health records accreditation board which awards the accreditation status.

The scheme is being broadened to incorporate a data quality audit. It is intended that three months before the survey, senior medical coders from other hospitals will spend some time re-coding

Table 2.1   South Western medical records

The standards cover many areas of hospital functioning which have an effect upon the service produced by health records but which are not directly concerned with records. For example, standard 5 says that the quality of service provided for patients by health records staff must be of a high standard, to include good communication and effective arrangements for their contact with health service staff. The criteria for assessing compliance with this standard are:
entrances to the hospital should be:

> close to car parks and bus stops
> clearly visible and well signposted inside as well as throughout the grounds
> readily accessible for both the disabled and able-bodied
> pleasantly furnished and regularly cleaned

a number of the records of the hospital being accredited to see if there are any discrepancies. The information collected is incorporated into the survey.

This self-assessment approach is popular with the NHS which has a shortage of people to act as surveyors (see Chapter 5) and an apparent inherent dislike of external inspection. Providers prefer to undertake reviews of their activities themselves and then discuss the results with external bodies.

Although not technically an accreditation scheme, there is a major competitor for accreditation in almost every health care market. BS 5750 as it is known in the United Kingdom (otherwise known as ISO 9001/2/3/4 or EN 29000) is a system for validating quality assurance systems. It sets out ways to establish, document and maintain an effective quality system which will demonstrate to customers a commitment to quality and an ability to supply their quality demands. Its emphasis on quality assurance has tended to cause comparisons to be made between it and accreditation. It is based on very similar premises to organizational accreditation. The nature and degree of organization, structure, resources, responsibilities, procedures and processes are essential management decisions affecting quality. It is as important that they are documented. The quality system must be planned and developed to take into account all other functions, such as customer liaison, manufacturing, purchasing, subcontracting, and training. It places a very different emphasis upon quality as it is concerned not with compliance with standards, but with the implementation of quality assurance processes (see Chapter 7).

Most accreditation processes focus upon the nature of the organization in which health care is delivered. In many cases, therefore, the standards concentrate on such things as the meeting of health and safety regulations, the correctness of administrative procedures, staffing and training policies, the existence of policies and procedures and the processes used to create them. A distinction needs to be drawn between 'creating the right standard' and 'creating the standard rightly' (see Chapter 7). It is the latter which is considered important in organizationally based audit. There is a generally held view that the content of policies and procedures, for example, are not questioned. It is their existence and use which is of importance for the audit. To this end the JCAHO standards now incorporate definitions of the dimensions of performance (see Table 2.2).

This focus raises the inevitable question of whether organization contributes directly to patient care. For some, organization is something which operates independently of patient care. In other models, organizational processes create the environment in which care is provided (Dunea 1982). This model suggests that patient care depends not only upon individual professionals but also the integration of systems. As explained above, not only is accreditation having to contend with these different models of health service structure, it also has to deal with the politics of professionalization. The more the standards move away from organizational issues towards clinical issues, the more difficult it is to get agreement about the content of standards, and procedures to assess compliance. The professional accreditation systems demand that only professionals can assess good practice, recognizing the implicit and unstatable diagnostic and treatment decisions involved. As whole hospital accreditation in the UK has been established by bodies other than professional ones, it is perhaps not surprising that the professions have retained a strong desire to keep accreditation of their practices separate from bodies such as the King's Fund.

Notwithstanding the resistance of the professionals to the concept of whole hospital accreditation, there is a growing interest in it. The new internal market of the NHS is encountering difficulties in dealing with issues of public accountability, and also in reassuring patients that standards are not falling. Accreditation, focused on the proper organization of hospitals and health services seems to offer a solution to these particular problems. But precisely how an

Table 2.2   Joint Commission dimensions of performance

Appropriateness	The degree to which the care provided is relevant to the patient's clinical needs, given the current state of knowledge.
Availability	The degree to which the appropriate care is available to meet the patient's needs.
Continuity	The degree to which the care is coordinated among practitioners, between organizations, and across time.
Effectiveness	The degree to which care is provided in the correct manner, given the current state of knowledge, in order to achieve the desired/outcomes for the patient.
Efficacy	The degree to which the care has been shown to accomplish the desired/projected outcome(s).
Respect and caring	The degree to which a patient, or designated other, is involved in his or her own care decisions, and that those providing services do so with sensitivity and respect for individual needs and differences.
Safety	The degree to which the risk of an intervention and the risk in the care environment are reduced for the patient and others, including the health care provider.
Timeliness	The degree to which the care is provided to the patient at the time it is most beneficial or necessary.

Source: Reproduced with permission from the Joint Commission on Accreditation of Healthcare Organizations, Copyright Joint Commission on Accreditation of Healthcare Organizations, Oakbrook Terrace, Illinois 60181.

accreditation system should operate within the internal market is still unclear.

PROVIDER INTEREST IN ACCREDITATION

A survey of 170 Trust chief executives, conducted during 1994, revealed a considerable level of interest in the concept of accreditation. It is clear from the responses that standards are now a very important part of health service activity. Three-quarters of the respondents were developing standards in-house for use in their own units and presumably nationally agreed standards would help in the derivation and use of such standards. However, the standards are more likely to be seen as helping with the development of clinical and professional practice rather than as instruments of quality assurance *per se*. Just under half the respondents felt that a national accreditation scheme could replace existing quality assurance schemes and clinical accreditation schemes.

In industry, participation in accreditation type schemes such as ISO 9000, the British equivalent being BS 5750, has been perceived as a useful marketing tool. This perception was clearly felt by a number of participants. Just over half felt that accreditation could be used to negotiate price within contracts, but this would require purchaser agreement. Of those who had participated in the King's Fund Organisational Audit, less than one-third felt that the purchasers had taken any notice of their participation to negotiate quality in contracts. But there are slight movements towards purchaser interest though this must not be assumed to be a permanent attitude. Some, albeit a small number, of the purchasers are beginning to appreciate the possible benefits of accreditation. One-quarter of the respondents who had been through the King's Fund exercise claimed that their purchasers had insisted on it. Obviously if more purchasers adopt such a policy of insistence, providers will undoubtedly be forced to go through accreditation type processes. In fact, 85 per cent of the respondents felt that accreditation should be paid for, either solely by the purchaser, or by the purchaser and provider jointly.

However, there are some complex issues in terms of the use of information provided by the accreditation process (see Chapter 5). Most accreditation reviews result in the writing of a detailed report which contains recommendations on how the participating organization could improve its internal management or service delivery. Interviews with chief executives who had participated in the King's Fund suggested that providers are reluctant to allow such information to go to their purchasers. It was generally felt that such information would encourage purchasers to dabble in provider management issues – something which providers feel is unacceptable interference in their work.

There is also an emerging view that standards should focus on good practice and service development, aimed towards optima rather than minima. This suggests that a model for controlling market entry is rejected by most respondents. The logical corollary of this is that respondents prefer some form of service development model rather than an 'inspection'. This is supported by two other findings. First, the majority of respondents wanted some form of continuous monitoring system rather than the traditional one-off surveyor visit associated with accreditation systems. Second, just under half the respondents felt that they would prefer a system of scaled grading rather than a pass or a fail. Less than 8 per cent supported the idea of a pass or fail basis for an accreditation system.

The independent or private health care sector has a different but equally valid set of reasons for wishing to see a new approach to assessing the quality of its provision. At present it operates under the controls imposed upon it by local health authorities responsible for the registration of hospitals. These are locally conducted and locally determined – with inspectors of variable quality, using variable standards and variable judgement. The lack of standardization of the approach and outcome has done little to assist the private sector to ensure that poor providers are flushed out, and that good providers can compare their performance, one to another and against their competitors within the NHS.

The private sector is looking for a more 'level playing field' upon which to operate. To compete fairly with the NHS it requires national standards. To compete fairly within its own sector, it also requires national standards. The solution facing them is to either depend upon one or a number of the many accreditation systems which exist, or to develop their own independent solution. The latter has many disadvantages, because it fails to achieve the desire to demonstrate cross-sector comparisons and would not be seen as a true and independent test of quality.

PURCHASER INTEREST IN ACCREDITATION

Why might accreditation be becoming an issue for purchasers? According to Challis *et al.* (1994) there may be a variety of motives. There is without doubt information asymmetry. The purchasers are at an information disadvantage. As time passes, they become increasingly distanced from the day-to-day work of providers. Their skills to judge quality are becoming limited. There is the difficulty, described earlier, that quality can only be described and indeed measured after the event. Switching costs to new providers may be very high, if not impossible in the short term, where the only solution to means of meeting the health care needs of a geographical population may involve building a new health care facility, or bringing in a new management team. Purchasers also may face a wide range of potential providers. Assessing the quality of all presents high transaction costs. A system which assesses quality nationally would reduce the burden on purchasers to develop their own systems of quality assessment and also, meet demands for equity across local populations.

It is clear that widespread accreditation processes will be central to quality assurance applied to patient care; paragraphs 67, 68 and 70 of 'Improving Health Care – a guide' clearly indicate that the Executive are interested in the development of appropriate registration of accreditation, and further that its existence may influence, or indeed enforce, the placing of contracts only with approved providers.

(McMahon and Winters 1993: 5)

Health authority purchasers and GP fundholders alike face the problems of defining and measuring quality. These difficulties are more acute for fundholders who have limited resources to assess the quality of care provided, and certainly to ensure that service environments are safe. The findings from a survey of 153 GP fundholders showed that a high proportion (over 59 per cent) were in favour of a national system of accreditation to support them in their purchasing decisions (Scrivens and Redmayne 1995). Of the fundholders who wanted a national system of accreditation, 90 per cent felt that this could replace the quality clauses in contracts.

It is of course equally possible that GPs in general might value the reassurance provided by accreditation. If it transpires, as it might, that GPs are, as the agents of the public, responsible for the quality of care provided to each patient, they may well wish some wider national system to take the burden of responsibility from their shoulders. To be able to argue in court that the hospital in question had been surveyed and the GP was acting in good faith when he or she referred the patient, might well be seen as an advantage. A purchaser perspective would be likely to push in favour of high standards. Indeed, of those who felt that accreditation could replace quality clauses in contracts, only 33 per cent wanted to see standards set at a minimal level which would act as guarantees of service. In contrast, 65 per cent were in favour of optimal standards which would reflect much higher service levels.

One argument in favour of accreditation is that it could replace, in addition to the duplication of quality assurance activity by purchasers, much of the other quality checking being undertaken by the Royal Colleges who accredit institutions and individuals for training purposes. The views of the medical profession in the UK are that they must control these activities and not surprisingly, less than 30 per cent of fundholders felt that a national system could replace existing Royal College accreditation systems.

Health authority purchasers had similar views. In a survey of purchasing district health authorities in England, 75.7 per cent of the respondents (75 per cent of the total number of authorities) felt that the NHS would benefit from a national accreditation scheme. The remainder who did not support the idea felt that such developments should be local or focused on specialized service areas. But only 46 per cent felt that a national accreditation scheme could replace many of the existing quality assurance schemes and clinical accreditation schemes; 86.6 per cent felt that the standards should be subject to external validation, that is, reviewed by professional or other NHS bodies and only 23 per cent felt that the standards should be set by purchasers; 51 per cent of responding district purchasers wanted standards to be optimal rather than minimal. The majority (61 per cent) wanted some form of continuous monitoring, rather than the survey visits, and 64 per cent wanted this to be compulsory.

This suggests a model much akin to the traditional methods of performance review with which the NHS is familiar, than an accreditation model. Their primary interest was in finding ways of monitoring contracts rather than reducing the complexities of contract writing – 84 per cent did not want to see accreditation replacing quality clauses in contracts. This may be due to the structural vested interests which are becoming an integral part of the reformed NHS. Removing the need for contract clauses would diminish the work of purchasing authorities and accreditation built into the purchasing process might well reduce the requirement for purchasing personnel.

Private health insurers are also becoming interested in accreditation. In the USA private insurers have frequently adopted JCAHO accreditation to determine which providers to support. The same pressures are being felt within the UK. Insurers face an ever-growing market of highly variable quality – including NHS owned private facilities. They are dependent solely upon the registration provided by health authorities, or by their own assessment systems. The private insurance companies face the difficulties of any purchaser, inexperience to judge quality, lack of resources and would prefer the comfort of third party professional endorsement. Furthermore, accreditation type gradings allow the potential pool of competing providers to be reduced as those that fail to get, or refuse to participate in, accreditation can find themselves ineligible for consideration by insurers.

CENTRAL INTEREST IN ACCREDITATION

The centre of the UK NHS in the form of the Department of Health and the NHS Executive, has many means to monitor the activities of its providers and its purchasers. But much hinges on the relationship between the centre and its peripheral agents. For many managers of the NHS, interviewed as part of the research into accreditation, the spectre of a central inspectorate, or an accreditation system created and controlled by the government, suggests a lack of trust in their work. Historically monitoring has been undertaken by internal reviews, of one higher hierarchical level or another or through the submission of statistical returns to the centre which are then analysed and published.

Although the breaking of the hierarchy has led to difficulties in determining the precise nature of accountability and how it should be monitored, many managers would argue they should be trusted to provide accurate reporting of their work. The centre of a national health service always faces a conflict. Ideally organizations would honestly and willingly submit themselves to external review to ensure public accountability. Ideally there should be means to compare performance, to establish norms of activity and to reassure the holders of the public purse that money is being well spent. The reality is that systems designed by the centre are seen as interference and systems promoted from the grass roots are rarely able to achieve national coverage.

There are two institutions which do operate nationally across England to check on the use of resources and the activities of NHS organizations: the Health Advisory service and the Audit Commission. These both suffer from the problems of being seen as central controllers, although both try to act in the model of promoting self-development and education. The Health Advisory Service, although limited to mental health and elderly services, offers one model of monitoring. It is

> a model of a professional-consultancy style of inspection which is so highly developed and self-conscious that it repudiates with some horror, the very idea that it might be called an inspectorate. It is an independent agency, though funded and

serviced by the Department of Health . . . Its 'inspectors' are
all professionals, temporarily working for the HAS.

(Day and Klein 1987b: 7)

Their role is to identify issues, and good practice to make recommendations about how the activities of individual organizations and
their practitioners can be improved. According to Day and Klein
(1990) its role is as a professional consultancy, coaxing and helping
to encourage service development, continuing the theme that inspection for the sake of inspection is not considered an acceptable
activity within the NHS.

The second obvious contender is the Audit Commission, set up in
1983, originally to ensure compliance with the law and to enforce a
set of accounting rules. Although the main activities of the Audit
Commission are to ensure proper arrangements are made for
securing the economy, efficiency and effectiveness in the use of
resources, their work has focused on helping local health services to
improve their performance by the spread of good practice. The
Audit Commissioners use auditors to protect the public interest, for
both probity and value for money. Because auditors come from a
different background with different skills, they are forced to use
audit approaches, developed within the Audit Commission to
identify poor practice and promulgate the good. Their complete
reports are private but the summaries, in the form of a management
letter, are made public.

These two very different models of external review, although
fulfilling important aspects of the public accountability agenda, do
not meet the needs of the service for explicit statements of good
practice. Nor do they enable a rigorous comparison of health
service activity. They are both the instruments of a central perspective on accountability. The accreditation systems which are growing
up start from a very different position. They are the product of a
provider-driven agenda – a concern to know whether they are doing
a good job. It is too easy to underestimate the isolation felt by
hospital managers about the day-to-day running of their services
and the potential risks that they face of not knowing everything
about the massive organizations they control.

Neither HAS nor the Audit Commission have agreed any rep-
licable standards. They cannot award gradings to show how well
one service is doing against another. Accreditation therefore provides a very different opportunity to fill a gap in the accountability
agenda, with support from the providers because it meets their

specific need for reassurance. It offers, in theory at least, a mid-ground between the inspectorial functions – although both argue they support education and organizational development – of the HAS and the Audit Commission. It attempts to meet local needs for reassurance about meeting good practice – against pro-fessionally established standards, and it enables a top-down view of how well one organization is doing against another.

Accreditation began as a form of self-regulation within the health care industry and retains its nature in the Canadian and Australian systems. Within the UK there are questions about whether self-regulation is the most appropriate mode of control of the health care industry. If Trusts are to be independent bodies, there is an argument for supporting that independence in having an equally independent body, supported by the professions of the health service who will question the quality of service provided by each Trust. This would provide an independent process of assess-ment, similar to audit, which checks the regularity of Trust be-haviour and acts in the public interest. It affords a degree of protection to a government, as it acts as an external arbiter of quality.

But there are always political risks to a government dependent upon independent third party assessors of health service quality: 'The term "accreditation" can be politically embarrassing in the UK since it implies judgement on the National Health Service' (McMahon and Winters 1993: 5). A critical assessment can fre-quently be used to argue that more resources are needed in order to provide adequate health care for a local population. Within the National Health Service, despite the proclaimed independence of Trusts and their management, the Secretary of State still owns the Trust hospitals. The Secretary of State is still, in theory, held re-sponsible by consumers and the public for the provision of ad-equate levels of service. The usefulness of third party assessment in controlling the Trusts will depend upon the distance, not only real but that perceived by the general public between the govern-ment and Trust management. If the public believes that Trust management is entirely responsible for quality of services, then the government can use accreditation assessments to apportion blame to those Trusts, or purchasers, which apparently fail to achieve compliance with the standards. But if the government is held to be ultimately responsible for standards of care, such criticism can be politically damaging.

The government is protected by the desire of the accreditation board to encourage self-development and organizational education. This encourages the accreditation system to keep its findings confidential to the organization being surveyed. But, should the accreditation system interpret its role as meeting the needs of a wider constituency, such as individual consumers, the results of accreditation surveys are likely to be perceived as public information. Their findings would be made public and thus the relationship between the accreditor and accredited would be changed.

In a society which is becoming increasingly concerned about responding to public opinion, accreditation is a useful tool. However, the assessments made by the accreditation system will vary depending upon the level of the standards which are set, and who is selected to undertake the assessment. Peer review suggests that the health services professionals themselves interpret what is acceptable and appropriate. However, there are views that professionals may not be entirely in line with what the public wants, or what policy makers feel is affordable or acceptable. There has to be compromise between the standards pursued by health service professionals, and the standards desired by other groups in society. There is an argument, therefore, that governments should develop appropriate mechanisms, structures or relationships to encourage systems which acknowledge public and policy interests.

There are also pressures being exerted upon the health care systems to force them to consider a more standardized approach to quality assessment. There is a growing belief among health care practitioners in the European Union (EU) that there will have to be quality controls over contracts which cross country boundaries and also those which are within country boundaries. There is a belief that this could be accomplished using BS 5750 or EN 29000. However, it transpires that the generation of standards by each hospital is likely to be too difficult and time consuming. Furthermore, if every hospital has its own standards and definition of the processes of health care, comparability between services will be impossible. The most cost- and politically-effective solution is to have a single set of standards (such as those used by an existing accreditation system) which are acceptable within the BS 5750 framework. The accrediting body could then be 'accredited' to license for BS 5750 as an outcome of successful accreditation.

Although the Anglophone model of accreditation is run by private bodies, there are a number of developments in the United Kingdom which are in effect government initiatives which resemble accreditation schemes, although not designed specifically for health services. It is not impossible for a government to run an accreditation system – indeed the Catalonian government did develop one (Bohigas 1984, 1985). But it seems unlikely that a government would be able, given the demands for public accountability, to adhere to the fundamental principles of accreditation, voluntarism and education.

ACCREDITATION AND THE RIGHTS OF CONSUMERS

A growing anomaly of the internal market, or indeed any public service system which promotes the concept of consumer choice, is that traditional definitions of accountability are up and down – following the old assumptions of hierarchic control. Consumer choice operates outside these lines. There is a current belief that consumers should be able, at the very least to demand standards of an acceptable level, and at the most, to have enough information to enable them to exercise a reasonable degree of choice in the marketplace. Whether choice exists in reality or not, consumers are pressing to know more about the services they consume. The gap in the accountability structures of the internal market relating to consumer empowerment could be met by a system of external assessment. In this case, the accreditation body becomes an agent of the consuming public as well as the hospital in question. In effect it cuts across the work of the other organizations which exist to promote broader public values of accountability such as value for money. Consumers, as opposed to tax payers have less interest in whether their tax money is being spent efficiently. Their concerns are more with effectiveness and access to the 'best' treatment.

The consumer therefore has two primary concerns. First, whether standards of care are optimal – the 'best' – and second, whether health care activities are comparable, if not of equal quality across the country. So the public expectation would be entitlement to the best known care anywhere in the country. Although this dovetails into the approaches of the Audit Commission and the HAS, in that consumers do not want to find that resources which could have been spent on health care are being wasted, the Audit Commission and HAS do not provide reassurance in the form which consumers can use. Their reports are not easily accessible and comparable and they do not offer easy to understand assessments of the quality of care. The accreditation approach fits more readily with the consumer concerns of readily defined standards and easily accessible information and providing reassurance, endorsed by a third party, that health care is safe and (possibly) effective.

The UK is not alone in its piecemeal development of accreditation. Italy, South Africa and the Netherlands are experiencing similar developments. Any government wishing to make progress on accreditation has to make choices between a number of options: the growing accreditation activity should be stopped or allowed to continue; accreditation should be left to develop as a system of quality control for provider interest only; or, accreditation should become part of the overall processes of quality control used by the national policy makers to reassure the public that health service quality is acceptable.

Like all forms of external review or inspection, accreditation is costly, time consuming and imposed external standards may prevent service development and innovation. It is less costly than inspection as health service practitioners may be used to undertake the assessment process. It also therefore affords an opportunity for the spread of good practice between institutions and provides the opportunity for education. Accreditation also encourages self-assessment by institutions and is therefore claimed to generate an interest in quality.

The NHS is confronting additional choices in its approach to the internal market and its regulation. A decision has to be made about whether there should be direct NHS Executive promotion of accreditation. This could involve either: a series of local accreditation systems or a national accreditation system. The uses to which accreditation could be put in the market place vary. Accreditation could be seen as a means of guaranteeing Trust conformity to acceptable standards. If national standards and a national system developed, accreditation could be directed at ensuring equity in quality of hospital infrastructure, or (depending upon the orientation of the standards) quality of care provided.

Purchasers could be encouraged to use accreditation systems (or one accreditation system) to ensure quality of infrastructure, or quality of service delivery. There are two approaches. Purchasers could be encouraged to use one (if a national system is selected) or a variety of different accreditation systems to guarantee that Trusts are adhering to standards. Purchasers could be required to insist that Trusts are accredited, either by one or from a number of accreditation systems. If pluralism in accreditation is also allowed to continue, there will be a need to monitor the overall performance (organizational as well as clinical) of health care providers.

The United States has taken 70 years to arrive at its present attitude towards accreditation. Although Canada and Australia have had less time, 40 years and 20 years respectively, there is growing acceptance of the concept. The UK National Health Service is poised to move towards some form of national quality system, be it based on principles of quality assurance or aimed at raising overall standards. The situation in the United Kingdom demonstrates a number of points concerning accreditation systems. It should not be assumed that accreditation can only focus upon organizational processes. Nor should it be assumed that organizations are not interested in developing their own accreditation systems. What the UK system demonstrates is the potential for accreditation to play a part in the marketplace of the NHS. The most important information upon which this decision has to be based is whether there is any value in the accreditation system – does it in fact have any significant impact upon the quality of health services?

3

THE ACCREDITATION EXPERIENCE

Accreditation systems tend to follow a common pattern of operations. Standards are issued to participating organizations, the organization makes adjustments to its practices to ensure it meets the standards and then surveyors visit to check on the degree of compliance with the standards. In the course of the research project, funded by the Department of Health, we were able to follow the experience of hospitals going through this process to establish what it feels like to be on the receiving end. Our various investigations have provided an opportunity to examine the experience of both the King's Fund Organisational Audit and the Hospital Accreditation Programme.

THE KING'S FUND ORGANISATIONAL AUDIT

The King Edward's Hospital Fund for London, an independent foundation whose mission is to improve the quality of management in the NHS, has developed the nearest thing to a national accreditation system in the United Kingdom. This scheme has evolved from an interest in the experience of other countries with accreditation. In the early 1980s the Fund sent a multidisciplinary team to look at the JCAHO system (Maxwell *et al.* 1983). The JCAHO standards were tried out by two pilot hospitals but this development laid fallow for a while. Later the Fund set up a process of peer review for a small number of hospitals, and adapted the standards from the Australian system. This developed into what is now known as the King's Fund Organisational Audit Scheme. This is a scheme which, although it incorporates advice from the medical profession and colleges, is not dominated by them. The 17 member board includes representatives from general practice, the United Kingdom Central Council for Nursing, Midwifery and Health Visiting, the Royal Colleges of Physicians, Surgeons, and Obstetrics and Gynaecologists, the Professions Allied to Medicine, the Institute of Health Services Management, the National Association of Health Authorities and Trusts, the Independent Healthcare Association, the National Association of Community Health Councils. In addition there are two consumer representatives, one from the National Consumer Council. And finally there are observers from the Royal College of Nursing, the Conference of Royal Colleges, the NHS Executive, and the Health Advisory Service.

This is the most extensive scheme in existence. Its clients are acute general hospitals and teaching hospitals, all large institutions with many beds and also many independent (private hospitals) which tend to be relatively small and specializing in elective surgery. The final reports are qualitative highlighting areas of good practice and deficiencies. Recommendations are made for improvements, but it has no graded outcome. The scheme is different from any others reviewed in the UK and abroad, in that survey managers are employed who help the organization with its preparation. Unlike all other accreditation systems, the Board does not assess the individual reports returned to participating organizations. The activities of the Board are restricted to the overall workings of the operation and the standards. The surveyors, usually three working for three days are health service practitioners, a doctor, a nurse and a manager. Hospitals pay a fee to participate – the scheme is run on a not-for-profit basis and is self-funding.

Because of its origins, the emphasis has remained on self-improvement: on professional peers learning from each other during the surveying process. This is reflected in the fact that the King's Fund audit does not award a pass or fail or attempt any sort of accreditation award or grading, following the visits of its surveying teams but merely reports to the hospital concerned about what it has found. Again, as the name of the scheme suggests, the main focus of the standards and the surveys is organizational process. There has been no attempt to integrate – as in the US, Canada and Australia – clinical audit into the standard setting process. Clinical audit, although much stressed in the 1991 reforms, remains an entirely separate activity (Kerrison *et al.* 1993). There has been no attempt, as yet, to introduce outcome indicators. Changes are, however, being planned: the

King's Fund Organisational Audit Scheme is about to adopt the accreditation label, to offer pass/fail awards and to revise its standards to emphasize patient outcomes.

Like its counterparts overseas, the King's Fund is also extending the scope of the services it covers. It is moving into other service areas, notably community hospitals and primary care services.

THE KING'S FUND ORGANISATIONAL AUDIT PROCESS

Hospitals contact the King's Fund Organisational Audit Unit and make an application to enter the organizational audit process. The growth in popularity of the audit means that some hospitals have to go on a waiting list until there is a slot available for them. But once accepted the hospital is then supplied with the manual of standards (see Chapter 4 for examples) and a coordinator from the King's Fund is assigned to the hospital to help it through the 12 months of preparation for the final survey. The manual is then issued throughout the organization to managers who set about involving staff and ascertaining whether the standards are met. A steering group is appointed from within the body of hospital staff who supply the necessary management controls and motivation for staff. To encourage staff to understand the process and to feel involved, most hospitals hold open meetings where the steering group can talk about the process and what is involved. The King's Fund encourages participating organizations to go through a mock survey a few months prior to the survey which enables the organization to see how well it is doing. After 12 months of preparation, the surveyors (usually three, a doctor, a nurse and a manager) then visit for about three days to review the hospital against the standards. A timetable is arranged for the surveyor visits by the hospital and all necessary documentation is sent to the surveyors a week before the survey.

The surveyors normally meet with the management team early on the survey day to introduce themselves and to discuss any issues. They are then taken individually to meet the relevant staff and to visit wards and departments. In the course of the visits, they discuss the standards with the managers and their staff, and discuss aspects of interest with any members of staff they meet. Normally a night visit occurs so that the night face of the hospital can also be seen. The surveyors write down their impressions and compliance with the standards as they go around the hospital and at the end of each morning and afternoon begin to compile their reports. On the evening of the final day of interviewing the surveyors work together to draft the outline of their report on the performance of the hospital. On the final day of the survey, the surveyors meet with the executive team and inform them of their detailed findings. Then there is usually an open, public meeting with any members of staff who wish to attend where the surveyors report their general impressions.

The coordinator takes the draft report away and within a few months, after approval by the King's Fund board, the report, with commendations for good practice and recommendations for improvement, is sent to the hospital. It is then up to the hospital what it does with the recommendations. Most will institute processes to encourage staff to act upon them. And after three years, the hospital then decides whether it wishes to repeat the process.

THE HOSPITAL ACCREDITATION PROGRAMME

The Hospital Accreditation Programme (HAP) was the first accreditation scheme to develop in the UK and in some ways is the only true model in that unlike the King's Fund it awards an accreditation status. Its clients are community hospitals which provide non-acute care (mostly nursing, rehabilitation and minor surgery), frequently to rural communities, who have restricted access to the large acute hospitals. The scheme was derived from the Canadian model and its standards were first published in 1988 (Shaw *et al.* 1988). It awards graded scores offering one or two years' accreditation, with the possibility of non-accreditation. The board which has membership comprising representatives of the Royal Colleges of General Practitioners, Anaesthetists, Surgeons, Obstetricians and Gynaecologists, and Nursing, plus the rehabilitation professions, the English National Board for Nursing, the National Association of Health Authorities and Trusts, the Institute of Health Services Management, the Community Hospitals Association, the British Geriatrics Society, the Independent Health Care Association and the Community Health Councils, awards the final accreditation score. Surveys take one day, are pre-planned and organizations have to prepare themselves for the process. The scheme is self-funding, with participants paying for the costs of the

survey. The surveyors (normally two are in attendance) are practitioners working in community hospitals or general practitioners
who review the process. The standards focus only on organizational
processes and make no attempt to incorporate clinical standards.
However, in line with all other accreditation systems, the scheme
has been updating its standards to emphasize linkages between
hospital departments.

THE HAP PROCESS

The survey process in the HAP is very similar to the King's Fund in
most respects (Hayes 1992). The community hospitals receive the
manual containing the standards six months before the survey is due
to be conducted. During that time, the hospital staff work on the
standards to assure that they conform with them. In many cases, the
hospital managers will contact colleagues in other hospitals to check
ideas with them. On the appointed day, two surveyors review the
hospital against the standards, meet with the staff to give their
general impressions at lunch-time and at the end of the day. The
surveyors then write their report and when this has been passed by
the HAP board and accreditation status decided upon, the hospital
is issued with a certificate and a report showing good practice and
recommendations for improvement. After one or two years (depending upon the status awarded) the hospital has the opportunity
to repeat the survey before accreditation lapses. This is therefore a
continuing process of examination.

THE EXPERIENCE

Interviews were conducted with the managers who had participated
in either of the schemes to ascertain the impact of the accreditation
process and the views of managers towards the process. The 17
managers interviewed for the HAP were managers of small community hospitals, ranging from 9 to 40 beds. The 27 managers taking
part in the King's Fund scheme were chief executives of acute
hospitals ranging in size from 200 to 600 beds. In addition, a detailed
study of two hospitals participating in the King's Fund scheme were
undertaken by members of the accreditation study research team.
A comparison of the views of managers from the King's Fund and
the HAP shows a remarkable similarity in the perceptions of the

experience. Whether the organization is a large acute hospital or a small rural one, the work involved, the stresses and strains caused on the organization and the benefits to be derived are reported as being nearly identical.

THE MOTIVATION TO SEEK ACCREDITATION

Although participation in accreditation schemes is theoretically voluntary, for most health service staff, the perception of the voluntary nature of participation is limited. The decision to apply lies in the hands of the chief executives of independent Trusts, although a small number felt that they had been forced into this by their purchasers. The managers of the community hospitals, who are part of a larger management organization rarely had the opportunity to choose not to participate.

> The Unit General Manager talked to the manager of the scheme and we were volunteered to sign up. The same manager had only just decided to go on the programme. We felt we were a flagship and would like to join.
>
> (HAP)

> We didn't apply. The previous locality manager decided it would be a good idea and applied. It was discussed with us. She 'sold' the idea to us.
>
> (HAP)

A number of managers felt that they wanted to enter the accreditation programme to compare the performance of their hospital with others. A recurrent theme is that hospital managers, of both large and small institutions feel isolated in their work and wanted to be able to compare their management with their peers.

> The reasons for going for it were two-fold. First there was a recognition that for the future there needed to be some sort of benchmarking and league tables. We wanted to influence that, so we needed to understand it, and therefore had to do it. It was an opportunity for the organisation to take stock. It is a good way of testing out whether the hospital was working as a hospital or had clinical directorates which caused the hospital to split up . . . There were many who felt there were some

benefits to show a wider audience. It would show that our hospital was a good place.

(King's Fund)

At the time, I think that the answer was merely that we would know where we stood. And on the side of the survey where we didn't expect to do well, we figured that would give us an action plan, an agenda to instigate improvements. It's independent and relatively inexpensive.

(King's Fund)

In addition, the larger hospitals saw it as means of controlling the conflicting demands placed upon them by a number of different purchasers.

There were two main reasons. One was, we pride ourselves on high standards and therefore we wanted to test the theory, if you will, against a nationally recognised scheme. And two, as a hospital that has a lot of purchasers who could all impose their own quality standards, we thought we could take the initiative . . . rather than responding to 15 different sets of criteria, we could just say, there, we've done it to an independent national standard.

(King's Fund)

PREPARING FOR ACCREDITATION

It is generally accepted that preparation for accreditation is onerous, at least the first time. It is also accepted that probably the greatest value of accreditation lies in the preparation. There was little difference in the responses, whether the hospital is small (some community hospitals are only ten beds) or large (acute units can have as many as 600 beds).

Really it allowed us the opportunity to self-assess, to see these are the standards, how far do we go to meet them, and where we don't what action will we take to put it right. In many ways, this caused a certain amount of grief, to tell the truth, because we were very honest.

(King's Fund)

We had to write policies for everything . . . we didn't possess any. We decorated the whole place purely for accreditation. In

their questionnaires each head of department had to identify
shortcomings and met to discuss what we could do. Some
things we just couldn't, but we tried to see what we *could* do to
meet the standards.

(HAP)

Many hospitals, particularly the small ones, did not have
information in the appropriate format. Most had been managing
with very little information and the requirements imposed by the
accreditation standards generated a lot of work. In both the King's
Fund and the HAP systems, the standards were cascaded through
the hospitals requiring staff in all departments to pull together the
information.

All the forms went out to the various members of staff. We had
to have the information from central sources with statistics
which we needed. Nevertheless the staff came up with the
goods and on the day were complimented on the information
we had managed to get together. There were 25 people
involved; nursing staff, catering, admin. More or less everyone
had something to do with the nurses. Medical staff were not
involved last year but this year I will give it to one of the
purchasers.

(HAP)

We involved all the nurse managers, all the clinical directors,
all the department heads. It took an awful lot of my time to
manage the dissemination of standards, actually physically
going through them. It was very time consuming – a lot more
than we were led to believe.

(King's Fund)

Therefore, a major benefit from the requirement to provide
information before the visit was that managers were able to review
and amend existing information systems. They reported some
surprises in the information they reviewed. It was apparent to them
that if they had not been required to provide the information they
would never have examined it. The information questions had
changed between years one and two of the programme and the
changes were felt to be a great improvement. The managers did
point out that collecting the information took a tremendous amount
of time and effort, which they often reported was very rushed.

The first time they were useful because I realised what I hadn't got. But it made a lot of work for me. I had to rush around and create things.

(HAP)

Motivating staff is a major management task. Many managers found that they had to work very hard to instil enthusiasm and interest in the staff. Much depended upon their approach to the exercise. Leadership from the top of the organization turned out to be very important in demonstrating the commitment to a quality initiative.

[Our staff were] not enthusiastic at all. There was a certain amount of feeling threatened – especially to start – when the standards were first seen and identified as unachievable.

(King's Fund)

Mixed: on the whole they found it an interesting challenge and rose to it. The value was more in areas where people found they weren't as good as they had thought after all.

(King's Fund)

All accreditation systems are dependent upon considerable amounts of data collection. This is partly due to the demands of the standards for policies and procedures, partly due to the laborious task of checking compliance with the standards. Any organization going through accreditation for the first time expends a considerable amount of energy galvanizing staff to find the information. The most activity went into the writing of documents and policies for the surveyors to examine. A major benefit of the accreditation visit was that it required the collation of policies and statistical information which in many cases had not been collected before. Managers reported that they had used accreditation to encourage team work between the staff in the hospital. It provided a useful opportunity for different departments to come together to discuss issues within the hospital. It was also vitally important that the staff owned the accreditation process.

In particular, the doctors found it hard to accept the process. Many were very resistant to it and were not interested in getting involved. And without medical support, the exercise is of limited value. However, most managers found that by running special workshops, using notice boards and news letters for communication, and showing enthusiasm, that staff including the clinicians, could be won round.

> We had to do lots of presentations to staff to get them to take part. We had a notice board. We had to organise a special meeting for the King's Fund to come up and meet the medical staff. The doctors felt they couldn't understand what it was about and wanted convincing.
>
> (King's Fund)

THE STANDARDS

As the accreditation systems have attempted to cover the whole range of hospital (and health service) activity, the standards have multiplied in number, resulting in literally thousands of standards. But they do offer a definition of good practice and a starting place for assessing the quality of organizational processes for most staff who would find it difficult to decide the components of good practice.

> It is like going to an encyclopedia. You have to be bothered to look. You might not agree with all of them but they are good thought provokers.
>
> (King's Fund)

All the accreditation systems, including the King's Fund have found it necessary to revise the standards continuously to reflect new views of health care and service design. The rapid pace of change in the health service demands a lot of an accreditation scheme to keep it up to date and relevant to those delivering the services.

THE SURVEY VISIT

The value of the accreditation survey visit is the linchpin of success for accreditation systems. The surveyors, in effect, make or break the accreditation process.

> The two who came were delightful. They made every member of staff feel very comfortable and not threatened. They were very positive about the whole day and that was important. I felt I could go out and tell my girls 'well done'. They had put their

utmost into it and the way information was asked of them really
helped them.

(HAP)

It was the Spanish Inquisition. The GP surveyor was very
complimentary and made good suggestions but his manner was
inquisitorial and efficient. The Nurse was a bit warmer. We
were told they wouldn't get in the way but they took a lot of
time. The sister in casualty and the midwifery superintendent
were absolutely shattered afterwards. The domestic and
catering assistants weren't asked anything although they were
all prepared to talk. They were very disappointed about this. I
don't know what we would have done if there had been an
emergency.

(HAP)

The surveyors were very fair, accommodating, personable
people – and it is important that they do have the credibility
themselves as individuals.

(King's Fund)

All systems have found that the credibility of the surveyors is
crucial to the success of accreditation. If the surveyors are not of
high enough status, if they are not well qualified or if they appear to
make irrelevant comments or ask the wrong questions they can
bring the whole process into disrepute.

The one who didn't go down very well was the private
manager. He'd worked in the NHS for a very long time before
he went to a private firm, but unfortunately, because of his
private sector experience, he didn't have the credibility.

(King's Fund)

We felt that by and large the survey team were not up to the
job, in the sense that they came from much smaller organis-
ations. They didn't appreciate the political dimensions of a
large hospital.

(King's Fund)

We had problems with the nurse surveyor. She was a top
manager but she told the managers that the nurses would
benefit from a standard cardigan. It blew her credibility.

(King's Fund)

The surveyors have to use their judgement to assess which areas of the hospital to concentrate their energies upon. They have only limited time to review the processes of highly complex organizations. In the case of HAP, an unsatisfactory final grading was frequently contested by the participants who felt that they had not been reviewed objectively.

> If you look at it [the report] you can see that we were marked quite highly . . . got mostly credits. So what criteria did they use that we should not have been accredited? We felt on the whole we'd done quite well. It's all a question of judgement isn't it? But I think this hospital was actually much better than another I know that got two years' accreditation.
>
> (HAP)

The UK, with its less well developed commitment to accreditation, demonstrates a greater degree of scepticism about the value of surveyors. A number of hospitals have preferred to 'go it alone', obtaining the standards and limiting their involvement to self-assessment. There are different views about the benefits to be derived from this approach. It seems unlikely that the organization can inspect itself as adequately as others can. It is harder to structure the exercise and the process and requires considerable self-discipline. It is also impossible to gain the credence given by an external assessment.

The UK also shows the substantive difference in the experience of accreditation according to the size of the organization. The community hospitals reported that the survey day was a nerve-racking experience. Everyone said how tired they had felt at the end and experienced a feeling of anticlimax. Their main concerns were that the surveyors did not talk enough to the staff who had become very involved in the preparation for the day and had wanted to participate. And that sometimes the surveyors missed pieces of information which gave the impression that some things were not being done when they were. This reveals the highly personalized nature of the survey to a small hospital where accreditation was felt to be a 'family affair'. The same feelings were reported by the smaller private hospitals which had been through the process.

This contrasts significantly with the experience of the larger hospitals. The chief executives claimed that the surveyors disappear into the fabric of the hospital to emerge days later. Many staff did not even know the surveyors had been around. Although the standards applied may be identical, and the surveyor's approach the

same, the reaction of the institution may be very different. And staff
are 'hyped up' to the survey visit and have expectations which
frequently exceed the surveyors' ability to deliver, in terms of
meeting and talking with everyone.

> I think there was a great deal of build-up to the survey. We
> pointed out to them not to be disappointed if they didn't spend
> a lot of time in their area. But they were.
>
> (King's Fund)

> The general view was that it was less than we expected. At the
> end of the day it was a bit of a let down . . . not so much in terms
> of the work that went into it, but in the survey week.
>
> (King's Fund)

> It wasn't the most pleasant of days. When they left it was like a
> wedding day without the disco.
>
> (HAP)

> There was a tremendous anticlimax. Even though we prepared
> people to see organisational audit as ongoing, the surveyors
> came and then they were gone. Some departments had done
> remarkable amounts of work, and on the day itself, there was a
> fleeting visit. They didn't even see the surveyors, some of
> them.
>
> (King's Fund)

For the community hospitals, where the hospital had been referred for a future visit, or the accreditation status awarded was less
than the maximum number of years, the managers felt they may
have been unfairly judged by the surveyors.

REPORTS AND RECOMMENDATIONS

The final report which communicates the findings in written form
are equally contentious. The level of detail contained in the document is an important finale to the survey visit. The HAP experience
was that a number of the managers felt that they were too short,
particularly in cases where the hospital had been referred. Managers felt that the reasons for the accreditation status awarded were
not explained well enough. Many of the managers therefore spent a
considerable amount of time trying to reason out why they had not

received a two year accreditation. This was significant in the cases of managers who had encouraged their staff by telling them they were 'going for gold', for two year status. They felt they needed information to explain to their staff what had gone wrong. Not surprisingly, those who had received two years' accreditation were less interested in the fine detail of the report. But if there is a duty of education placed upon the accreditation programme, it is vitally important that final reports are accompanied by explanation and suggestions for improvement.

> The report sets out an action list. You have to agree what you are going to do and put dates on which they will be done by.
>
> (King's Fund)

The distribution of the report around the participation organization varies, often depending upon the result conveyed and the reactions of the staff to the accreditation status awarded. A number of the managers in the community hospital scheme confessed to having waited a while after receiving the report before telling staff its content. The King's Fund managers although not pressured by accreditation status, behaved in a similar fashion. There was a reluctance to make departmental managers feel that they were being criticized for their performance. So reports and recommendations were divided up, with only the relevant sections being handed to individual managers.

> Very, very useful. The report has been a bible . . . everyone's had it and knows what we must look at. Always being mindful that the GP and nurse who wrote it were not infallible. It's been a very useful tool for managers to enhance the quality. Very nice to go to the Trust with the report in hand and point out what's been highlighted as not so good.
>
> (HAP)

External reviews do raise expectations among the staff which cannot always be met. Not only do they expect to be talked to during the visit, they also expect consistency between the verbal reports and the final written report. Managing participating organizations' expectations turns out to be one of the hardest tasks.

> We did encounter one problem. . . . We had surveyors who visited a few directorates and they made their verbal report although they didn't mention it in the final written report.
>
> (King's Fund)

Some departments were left out of the written report and were fed up with the fact that they felt ignored and we had some serious morale problems after that.

(King's Fund)

THE PARTICIPANTS' PERCEPTIONS OF THE BENEFITS OF ACCREDITATION

Whatever the size of the organization, the preparation for at least the first accreditation visit appears to take considerable time and work. The organizational standards demand policies and procedures which, in many cases have to be decided and written. Much depends upon the desire of the managers to write usable policies. The greater the concern about applicability, the more necessary it is for managers to gain the interest and cooperation of staff. So in some organizations, the process of applying for accreditation becomes one of involving staff and gaining their commitment to the idea of quality and its implementation. The participation in accreditation systems therefore becomes more of a management tool and takes as many resources as managers wish to use.

The process of self-examination, that X factor with purchasers. It helped impress the staff that we are each very responsible and accountable for what we do and we must be open to external audit.

(King's Fund)

It helped us focus on quality. It would have taken us a lot longer to have a 'culture of quality' in the organisation. It was a good vehicle to provide us with an overview.

(King's Fund)

It recognised the need to get clinicians involved in the process. It galvanised the staff to think about quality issues. It did make them update policies and procedures. It did get people to work together.

(King's Fund)

There are simple benefits in having an external review to reassure managers that the organizations are performing satisfactorily.

They didn't tell us anything we didn't already know but it was good to hear it from the King's Fund.

(King's Fund)

In the small community hospitals of the HAP scheme, accreditation forced the managers to look at the whole of the hospital rather than at discrete departments or functions within the hospital. A number of the managers were new in post and they felt that working through the accreditation process had helped them get a feel for the managerial tasks and responsibilities they were facing. In the larger hospitals participating in the King's Fund, the managers were more likely to have greater experience. For them accreditation served the purpose of creating a more coherent focus on quality for their staff. It became a symbol of commitment to quality initiatives.

The attitude of everyone is we must keep up the good work. Can't leave anything until next year. It's got to be continuous. Some things were out of our control; for example we were lacking a regular visit from a Pharmacist . . . now we have a regular weekly Pharmacist's visit. That's beneficial to everybody. The CHC is starting to make regular visits to the hospital about once a year.

(HAP)

Another benefit of accreditation, found in all schemes, is networking and support between managers in different hospitals. Entering the programme gave managers a reason to contact colleagues in other hospitals. Not only did this produce a sense of collegiality among participants, fostering new friendships and generating an excuse to visit other sites, it also alerted managers to good practices which were growing up in other hospitals. Interestingly, in the smaller hospitals there was no sense of competition between the hospitals but a growing sense of camaraderie. The competitive element was supplied by trying to achieve the status of two year accreditation. In fact a number of managers were distressed that their colleagues in other hospitals had failed to achieve the two year status. There were stories of visits to other hospitals to learn how to organize the day and make the appropriate preparations, of borrowed curtains, and advice on how to keep the surveyors happy – such as feed them a good lunch. The larger hospitals in the UK, facing greater competitive pressure, did tend to look further afield than nearby hospitals.

The difference between the impact of accreditation upon the

community hospitals and the larger acute units is striking in the UK. To a large extent this must be dependent upon the nature of the market they are facing, thus reinforcing the idea that accreditation can serve different purposes. The managers frequently perceived accreditation as a management tool. The external 'threat' of outsiders reviewing the hospital had created a sense of teamwork and coherence within the hospital which had been lacking before. Staff from all departments could be involved in preparing for the accreditation visit and could take ownership of the process. In addition this heightened their interest in the hospital and in making it successful.

The managers of the large acute units were less likely to 'sell' accreditation on this basis. They emphasized the need to make it a non-threatening exercise, encouraging staff but not allowing failure to be seen as criticism or failure. But care must be taken in interpreting these differences. One interpretation is that the community managers were protected from the need to consider competitive strategy by their relatively lowly place in the strategic hierarchy. But, the community scheme carries with it accreditation status and therefore the risk of failure is inherent within the accreditation process. The managers could not ignore the fact that their organization was to be judged and might be found wanting. The King's Fund at that time, did not have an accreditation score and therefore did not convey the same message to participants. The worst that could happen was criticism of the management and organization.

One recurring issue raised by managers across both the community and the King's Fund schemes, was that the surveyors made recommendations which require expenditure and in many cases the hospital did not have resources to make the recommended changes.

> In some areas they couldn't implement actions and felt it wasn't any use. Others couldn't be implemented because there was no money. . . . At the end of the day, if the report means money, we know we can't achieve it.
>
> (King's Fund)

In a number of cases, particularly the community hospitals whose managers have limited powers and even more limited budgets, this caused the managers to question the usefulness of the exercise: 'What is the point of being told to do things you cannot do anything about?' However, a number of community hospital managers saw a main purpose of the accreditation process as putting information to unit managers about the need for improvements and a means of arguing for more resources. Some managers felt that the surveyors should convey this information directly to senior management in order to ensure that the information had the desired impact. Equally a number of acute unit managers saw opportunities from the recommendations of the King's Fund to argue with their purchasers for more resources. The King's Fund outcome was seen as a vindication of management difficulties, enabling greater discussions between the purchasers and providers about capital investment and service development.

The positive effects of being told you are good enough were felt to create signals not only inside but also outside the hospital. The general public could be informed of the success of their local hospital.

> We put it in the local paper. We sent copies to the Community Health Council and the purchasers; but we don't think the purchasers noticed.
>
> (King's Fund)

Purchasers, too, in theory could be told of the relative success of their providers. Such is the theory. The community hospitals, frequently under threat of closure, were able to use a successful accreditation outcome to inform the general public of the tragedy of closure.

> It would be logical for all the hospitals around here to be accredited but we ought to know the reasons why not. It leaves a feeling of disappointment – if your hospital is accredited for two years it takes a lot of the pressure off. One hospital was very worried it would be closed. But since it got accredited the staff feel it can't be closed. This has a major effect on how people work.
>
> (HAP)

The larger hospitals were less likely to adopt such a strategy. Again, probably because the King's Fund did not carry any convincing measure of success. Furthermore, the larger hospitals also discovered the need to have a purchaser interested in, and capable of understanding accreditation. Although in a few cases the purchasers were asking for accreditation, few were interested in the results *per se*. The provider units accused their purchasers of ignorance of the purpose and the processes of accreditation.

We sent a copy of the report to the purchaser – the GPs were told too. There was a total lack of interest.

(King's Fund)

But, it was also the case that most providers were unwilling to share the reports emanating from accreditation with their purchasers. They feared that purchasers would seize upon recommendations and begin to use them to control the work of providers. This ambivalence can be attributed to the poor relationships most acute unit providers have with their purchasers in the internal market. The providers' greatest fear was that of interference from purchasers in their day-to-day management. Accreditation reports in many cases were too detailed to be shared with purchasers.

THE MANAGERIAL BENEFITS OF ACCREDITATION

First, accreditation systems provide standards against which organizations can be measured and can measure themselves. These may be perceived as the most important part of the accreditation system. The existence of standards offers guidelines for staff to match themselves against. They may also encourage staff to achieve them, reorganizing their work and reassessing their methods of practice.

Second, the presence of the surveyors creates an external check on standards which can encourage staff to improve their practices. The motivation to comply comes from a number of different sources: the need to belong, fear of letting colleagues down, fear of failure, an innate desire to do better. Our research suggests the motivation is fostered by the attitude of managers towards the accreditation process. The visit by surveyors can be interpreted to staff as a process of professional development or threatened as an inspection. In some cases, surveyors may perceive their role as reassuring staff that they are well on the way to achieving the necessary standards.

Third, the surveyors can act in a management development capacity, helping organizations achieve standards or higher standards, by advising them of the existence of good practice and highlighting the existence of poor practices.

Fourth, standards with interpretation from surveyors can help managers to detect areas of potential risk. Risk can fall into a number of categories, for example, clinical, financial and physical.

Table 3.1   South Western – examples of detected safety hazards

---

Policy and administration
Admission and discharge policies: lack of agreed definition of appropriate
patients (and thus equipment, staff skills and organization required).
GP contracts: many doctors working in hospitals (casualty or bed-fund)
have no contract with the health authority or trust.

Clinical services
Patient identification: lack of bracelets.
Medical records: lack of admission assessment, follow-up notes,
signatures.
Resuscitation: equipment ill-maintained; insufficient training in use of
equipment (particularly medical staff); call out procedure not organized.

Environmental services
Domestic/catering: lack of training for new staff in hygiene and safety;
policies unclear on saving food specimens in case of suspected infection.
Fire: blocked fire exits; unsafe storage; lack of fire officer reports.

Source: Reproduced with permission from The South Western Hospital Accreditation Programme

Here the surveyors can use the standards to diagnose problems in
organizational structures and processes which may put the organization and its patients at risk.

The risk management approach of accreditation may well be the
single most significant use for accreditation in many health care
systems. Rather than emphasizing quality as maximizing professional practice, it may be better viewed as a process of minimizing damage to patients. In all the systems, the most common causes
for the boards to withhold accreditation are concerns about safety.
The HAP scheme in the United Kingdom has analysed the reasons
why accreditation was not awarded to 16 per cent of the hospitals
which took part in its scheme. Examples of the potentially hazard-
ous impact of hospitals on patients and staff found in the HAP
accreditation scheme are listed in Table 3.1.

> These findings should not be seen to detract from the hospitals
> which volunteered to take part in the accreditation pro-
> gramme; indeed there is no evidence that any adverse events
> have resulted directly. Rather, it demonstrates the opportuni-
> ties which exist for reduction of risks and which may well apply
> to other, larger hospitals. Most of these issues require clear
> policies and organisation, rather than substantial extra money.
> (Shaw and Hayes 1992: 2)

One purpose of accreditation may be therefore to spread good practice. Ironically another may be to prevent too many deviations from occurring – to ensure equity in quality of care if not treatment across the service. There is a market based argument which says let the market choose and the 'best' (at least in terms of most appropriate accreditation system) will win. The expensive, time-consuming, disruptive systems will be ignored by the market and will wither and die. This will undoubtedly depend upon which players in the marketplace have the power to define the aims and objectives.

Perceptions of the standards are also important. Standards are the core of an accreditation system, and the choice of standards, their focus and the level at which they are set is crucially important in determining the tone, acceptability, and nature of the system (Scrivens (ed.) 1995). It has turned out to be almost impossible to devise workable standards without reference to the availability of resources. Whether staff feel it is reasonable to be asked to implement the standards will depend to an extent upon their views of acceptable practice within the resource constraints of the service. Furthermore, there are problems in validating some of the standards in that it is not clear that they in fact relate to clinical outcomes at all. In many cases the standards are derived from collective perceptions of good practice and rarely are or can be directly related to outcomes.

Assessment against the standards can be undertaken by a variety of agents. Those working within the organization, outsiders from within the health service, or outsiders acting on behalf of an external body. Again, the tone and nature of the accreditation scheme will be affected by two questions. On whose behalf are the external agents acting, and what decisions hang upon their findings? A number of managers have suggested that the main criterion for assessing the effectiveness of an accreditation system is the satisfaction of the staff with the process. There are a number of additional influences which need to be taken into account in any evaluation. The degree of success of accreditation, however defined, will be affected by, for example, the credibility of the surveyors. If staff feel that the surveyors are not being fair in their judgements, their perceptions of the process will be affected. Furthermore, the use of accreditation as a means of comparing organizational or service behaviour will be highly dependent upon the degree of consistency across the surveyors in applying their judgement. Any such comparisons will be compounded by the difference in environments, external, physical and managerial, in the institutions studied.

An important factor in the success of an accreditation system is the willingness of individuals to participate and to heed the verdict of the surveyors. If any part of the accreditation process is found to be unacceptable to those participating, it will be unable to achieve the required response. The implementability of the standards and credibility of the surveyors are both equally important in persuading participants to take the process and its recommendations seriously.

Although perceived benefits are important in determining the acceptability of the accreditation process they do not show categorically that any change has taken place in the delivery of health care or its outcome. However, the search for objective proof must be approached with caution. In our review of accreditation systems, we have asked managers with experience of organizational accreditation systems whether they would realistically be able to identify any changes detectable by indicators or measures. They all reported that the accreditation system was not designed to achieve this. Its impact was only to be expected in terms of attitudes towards quality or cultural change within the organization. Not surprisingly perhaps, the impact of the accreditation process is perceived to be confined to the original orientation chosen for accreditation.

Organizational indicators are limited to expected adoption of the standards such as the writing of policies and procedures. But are these in reality adopted by staff? Do staff understand and use the policies or do they simply sit on shelves gathering dust while practice moves ahead? Is the significance of the preparation for accreditation merely the production of documents or the internalization of the documents? If so, how do we measure whether staff have changed their practices in order to conform to the agreed policies? It often transpires that the examination of policy documents results in rewriting the policy to conform with current practice rather than changing practice. So perhaps the main advantage of accreditation is to bring policies into line with practice. This is not to be dismissed as a bureaucratic irrelevance. In health care systems where hospitals or their staff can be sued for malpractice, having explicitly written stated policies is an important part of risk management. So if the purpose of accreditation is to ensure that the organization is operating on sound administrative principles, this would be a desirable outcome.

I believe that if the organisation works better, the outcome will be better for the patient. The more effective the organisation is to underpin clinical issues, the better the clinical practice will be. We have evidence from patient satisfaction surveys. We can get into outcome measures in terms of patient satisfaction.

(King's Fund)

I can't see it has done anything for our bottom line. I suspect it has done something for the quality of service, the impact of staff on patients, that it's improved the speed and quality of our processes, improved our 'user-friendly aspects' – all the soft things that are hard to quantify.

(King's Fund)

I'm more interested in looking over the longer term at the behaviour of people inside the organization, but there are behaviours that we can check.

(King's Fund)

The more sophisticated challenges are those which address the outputs of the clinical process. Here there is an attempt to find changes which have occurred as a direct result of the organization going through the accreditation process. Outputs, however, being indicators which rarely relate directly to the process under study, require a causal or linking logic to suggest why they might demonstrate change. The collective understanding of the impact of the health care process upon patient health, commonly referred to as outcome measures, is developing but still limited. There are few satisfactory indicators which could be categorically related to the introduction of accreditation systems.

THE EFFECT ON STAFF MORALE

The way in which managers used accreditation as a tool to create interest and enthusiasm for change within the hospital undoubtedly had an effect in boosting staff morale when what was perceived as a good result was achieved. One of the most significant effects of outside evaluators examining a service is that staff expectations are built up and managers in the HAP scheme found that they faced serious motivation problems if the outcome of the evaluation is not what they have led staff to believe will occur. Without doubt, the prospect of accreditation created a feeling of enthusiasm and excitement which the managers were able to use to create changes. But the way in which accreditation was presented to the staff could have a serious and sometimes devastating effect on staff morale. Some managers presented accreditation as a competition with two years as the goal. This meant that those who did not receive a two year accreditation were inevitably seen to have failed. Managers reported difficulties in maintaining staff enthusiasm when the hospital had 'failed' the first time around.

Although accreditation schemes rarely refer to hospitals failing, preferring instead to talk about referrals or deferrals of accreditation status, much of the language of the managers related to passing and failing. In the HAP scheme even one year was seen as failing and this was obviously conveyed to the staff.

> At the end of the day we were all fairly happy . . . just thought we would await their decision. We felt we had shown them a nice little hospital. Then we waited three months to be told we hadn't got accredited. Then we felt disappointed.
>
> (HAP)

In the South West, when an accreditation status had been received, the managers found they also faced motivational problems because the staff could become complacent, feeling that the process was easy and did not require additional work. As seen above, the accreditation systems have to work hard to find ways to maintain interest and enthusiasm over time. Furthermore, the HAP scheme demonstrated the problems of an accreditation scheme which made recommendations which managers felt they could not implement. In the UK system there was a greater propensity for managers to feel that they would cease participation in the scheme as there was no point in applying for something that could not be achieved.

This highlights the dichotomy within many accreditation schemes about their duty of public accountability against meeting the needs of their individual client organizations. Managers argue that there are some aspects of hospital activity over which they have little control. But the managers who perceive themselves to be in this position feel they are continuously faced with the prospect of never improving their accreditation status and this made a mockery of accreditation. They also felt that in cases where they were only awarded one year accreditation, they were being fined by having to pay an annual revisit fee. Another example from the HAP scheme shows another dimension of this problem. A common recommendation was that medical audit should be introduced. UK community hospitals rarely have medical staff, using independent general practitioners when they need medical inputs. A similar experience occurs in private hospitals which do not employ medical consultants. It was felt by a number of managers to be impossible to introduce medical audit where GPs had refused to take part. They repeatedly pointed out that they have no managerial control over the GPs and if they do not wish to do something a hospital manager is not in a position to force them. Again, it could be argued that a good manager will find a way around this problem. It is a test of good management to find solutions for what are seemingly intractable problems. But is the role of accreditation to test for good management skills in this way? To what extent is management inextricably linked to the successful running of a hospital or health care provider?

THE ROLE OF ACCREDITATION

There are considerable differences in the perception of the role of accreditation. The interpretations vary from a badge of achievement, to a management tool to create change, to an opportunity to check on standards, or a continuing process of achieving quality improvements. The UK experience shows that where criticism was directed at the programme it normally stemmed from the assumptions about the role of accreditation. Many of the HAP managers referred to 'not getting accreditation' suggesting they saw it very much as a pass or fail exercise with all the associated difficulties of maintaining high levels of staff morale when a two year status was not awarded. A number of managers felt that they did not understand precisely what the surveyors were looking for and said that they had experienced great difficulty in explaining a disappointing outcome to staff. There were a number of different interpretations of the accreditation status awarded. A high proportion of the managers saw two years as the goal to be aimed for, and therefore anything less than that was frequently perceived as failing to succeed. This caused considerable heart searching to find out what they 'had done wrong'. Most were looking for some omission.

There was a considerable amount of emotion attached to accreditation status. A number of managers felt it was a means of staving off possible closure and therefore failure was perceived as a threat to the long-term viability of the hospital. Often, where the managers could not explain the outcome, especially compared with nearby hospitals, they questioned the variation in the surveyors' judgement either between surveyors or between surveyors over different visits. Others blamed the board who make the final decision feeling that they do not understand how community hospitals work.

Acute hospitals had different views.

Accreditation ought to be about developing a gold standard – we are a national health service. If you walk into a hospital in London or Liverpool, there should be a certain standard neither falls below – all should be about equal, there's a guarantee, you know what to expect.

(King's Fund)

One is to satisfy yourself internally that you have systems in place to manage, monitor, set standards etc. That they are in place. And then it's to be able to influence the market that we're worth buying from because we have got a kitemark. Someone from outside has said we're OK, we're safe, we're good quality.

(King's Fund)

Two reasons. One is to reassure our customers in a genuine and objective way as to the quality of the service we are providing. Two, to make us think seriously, and to challenge us, about quality.

(King's Fund)

There should be a standard that all hospitals achieve, and the purpose of accreditation is to see that people achieve it.

(King's Fund)

Another issue was whether the accreditation visit should be a random spot check or whether it should be, as it is currently, a visit for which the hospital prepared in advance. The supporters of the former view suggest that the surveyors ought to examine the hospital as it runs. The supporters of the latter view feel that the right staff can be asked to come in to be there to answer questions and to explain the workings of the hospital.

I think the benefits would be less artificial if it was a spot issue. People prepare their hospitals for an accreditation visit but in six months will the problems reappear? At the end of the day we would be getting policies together, picking up fag ends the process is taking over. But even so there are some areas which we need to work on. It is difficult to look at the picture and it is helpful to have someone to spend a day with you. It gives you a set of targets to achieve. Overall one should improve and staff are told this. People do get a buzz from working in a four star hospital.

(HAP)

I don't think a spot check would work. We wanted the information and the key people there who would be happy to give their views. You have to set aside time to talk to the surveyors. The present system is reasonable. It's their impressions that count. They are not looking at the day-to-day running but the standards which had been running all the time. If you had all new care plans they would know it. They are not stupid – even if we would like to think they are.

(HAP)

Another issue raised by many of the managers was the time between the surveys. A number who had been awarded a one year accreditation status felt that no sooner had they received the results of one survey than the preparation for the next visit started. Those who approached accreditation as a continuous pressure to improve standards were less likely to hold this view, but those who saw it more as a badge, something to show that the hospital had passed an examination, were more likely to feel that the visits were too close together.

Overall it is a good system but we ought to rework the one year business. Two years feels more like time to do something. There is no time – six months from getting the certificate you have to start again.

(HAP)

The visits are not really once a year. They are only six months apart and this is a very short time in order to make changes.

(HAP)

The King's Fund did not suffer from the same problems because, at the time of the survey their visits were not dictated by the accreditation status awarded. Instead they just revisited on a three yearly cycle. But the three yearly cycle presents problems. There is a tendency to put the reports on the shelf and forget the survey ever took place. For managers who were interested in using the process to change attitudes to quality, there were problems in finding appropriate mechanisms to continue the work started by the accreditation process.

> When you are having the survey you can galvanise people. But when its done, where's the impetus to maintain adherence to the programme?
>
> (King's Fund)

In some hospitals the steering group was retained, charged with the duty of implementing the survey recommendations. In others, internal forms of organizational audit were introduced to fill the gap between surveys. A group of senior managers took the place of surveyors to review departments' progress.

In both schemes the majority of managers interviewed felt that they wanted to continue with the programme, because the benefits of having outside assessors examining their hospital were great. A commonly used phrase was 'keeping everyone on their toes'.

> I must continue. I'm trying to get us accredited. The director of nursing says if the kitchens are fixed we'll go for it again. I think it is an excellent programme. I feel keen to be an assessor as well.
>
> (HAP)

> Yes – definitely and yes I want to continue. I don't know if the staff do. I think they are very sceptical now. It is a way of keeping everyone on their toes.
>
> (HAP)

> Yes, you have to do it again. It's pointless as a one-off. This was a baseline, really. We have to see, have we moved on?
>
> (King's Fund)

Even so, there were a number of chief executives who were questioning the need to repeat the King's Fund process, not because they did not achieve benefits but because the requirements of the organization might have changed in the future. To a large extent this reflects the self-education motif of the King's Fund, which may be very different under a true accreditation assessment.

> Doing it created a momentum. Having achieved the momentum, I would only go for further external review if I felt our

momentum needed a further external boost or if we received criticism that we were ducking something by not doing it.

(King's Fund)

This organisation has undergone a great deal of change in a very short period of time . . . a big, big cultural change, and I'm very nervous of imposing too much of a strain on the system. If we are going to do it, I want to do it in the right way and at the right time.

(King's Fund)

However, the impact of accreditation was felt more acutely in the HAP scheme. Those who had been referred were concerned that they would continue paying for an assessment when there was nothing they could do to improve the situation. Where staff morale had fallen to a low, the managers felt it was hard to motivate staff to participate.

There was a financial crisis so there was no money from the works department to upgrade the kitchen . . . no enthusiasm for anything. The hospital was very busy with staff sickness and low morale. After all it was a January visit. There was a feeling of 'why do it again if it will fail again?' Management are still changing and I've now lost control of the hospital to the locality manager. I've no real say any more because I'll no longer control the budget. The new locality manager is experienced with the NHS but from the community side but she has no experience or knowledge of small hospitals.

(HAP)

Another concern was the ability to pay for the programme. A number of managers felt that they could not afford to pay out of their budget and indeed some had been told that their Trust managers had decided they could not afford to continue.

We would like to but I've just been told today that there aren't the funds to continue. Last time the health authority paid. Now they are a Trust. The chairman for the Trust says that she has talked to the accountant and there isn't the money available which is really rather sad. If the money was available I think I would be required to continue.

(HAP)

I feel if you haven't got motivation and leadership at the top you really need someone to pull it all together. If you have apathy at the top you have it right through the organisation. You have to put work into accreditation, there's no point entering it if you're not prepared to work hard. Hard work means updating things . . . not letting standards slip having achieved them once. Don't think accreditation for three years is a good idea because standards will drop. You need to constantly review what you are doing. There is no point in it if you don't have to raise your standards.

(HAP)

The issue of payment influenced all managers' perceptions of the accreditation programme. Most assumed it was paid for by the unit, but those who had faced the bill themselves felt that they had to think very carefully about the value of accreditation. The most common complaint from those who had only received one year's accreditation was that it was an expensive process if it was going to be repeated every year. A two year accreditation status effectively halved the annual bill for the survey.

It is very expensive when you know it will only be for one year. It will be over £1,000 and if we are going to be for one year it is a lot. We hoped the centre would pay. I authorised the payment and we got the bill months later. We tried to get reimbursement from the district but they were not interested because we asked them to pay it. But you can always think of other uses to which you can put the money. It is the equivalent of eight mattresses.

(HAP)

I don't think it is worth the money because we had good standards. If your standards are poor then you are paying to keep being referred. If it was every two years we could live with the cost. I will review the idea every two years but if we only get one year then we won't bother again.

(HAP)

Few managers wanted to stop the process but a number were concerned that they could not afford the price with ever stretched budgets. The majority of managers felt it should be funded from a central budget, and a number felt it should be paid for by the purchasers, especially if they were demanding accreditation as a prerequisite for awarding a contract.

After the next time we will have to pay but I won't pay unless the money for it is found. I don't know who will pay next time

but it won't be us. We want reassurance that the money will be
made available to pay for it. We're not appropriately funded
for it. Would the purchasers pay for it if they want accreditation? I don't want to say anything about the future. It's such a
difficult question. I just want the best for this hospital. Perhaps
one would just have to be overspent on it. I feel cynical about
lots of one year accreditations at £1,000 a go. I am wary of who
gains by doing accreditations.

(HAP)

It's a bit unfair you have to pay for quality control. It should
come from general funds. If we failed we'd go on if we felt we
could achieve what we wanted. You'd lose heart if it was an
impossible goal. Like the first time with our old building. You
couldn't change it so you felt you were in a cleft stick. Then you
might not want to go on, it would feel like money down the
drain.

(HAP)

Accreditation began as a process of self-education but within the
internal market its role appears to be changing, in a way not
dissimilar to the USA experience. It is being seen more as a process
of quality control and assurance. This is certainly true when the
wider needs of the health service are examined. The private or
independent sector has a particular interest in the development of a
national accreditation system which tend much more towards the
need for an appropriate regulatory framework than simply for
individual hospital consumption.

THE INDEPENDENT SECTOR

Since 1987 the independent sector in the UK has been calling for an
accreditation system for hospitals. The reasons are four-fold. First,
there is a perception that accreditation may be a useful marketing
tool. Second, insurance companies are becoming increasingly interested in accreditation as a means of both checking quality of
providers and reducing the size of the pool of providers with whom
they could contract. Third, that it might enforce a 'level playing
field', not only for private providers reducing potential variability
between providers, but also between the NHS and the independent
sector – particularly as health authorities are allowed to widen the
base of their contracting to non-NHS providers. Fourth, health

authority inspectors, according to a survey report from the Independent Healthcare Association, were found lacking in experience and a national perspective, were hostile and rarely made suggestions for improvement (Feinmann and Davies 1987).

The independent sector has been reviewing a number of possibilities. Many subscribe to the pathologists' (CPA) accreditation or use laboratories which have been through the process. Investors in People has an appeal to a number because of its emphasis on training and business planning. BS 5750 is being tested by a number of hospitals. Although those that have experience found it a useful exercise many managers felt it was too bureaucratic and complex to operate successfully. In addition, BS 5750 is not wholly understood within the health care community.

The King's Fund is seen to offer a developmental approach which does push for the attainment of certain standards. The private sector has held hard to the notion that it needs a system which incorporates not only checking compliance with standards but which also enables the transfer of experience between the two sectors.

Obviously the independent hospitals are concerned about the price of the accreditation process, but if it is a useful marketing tool, for them, it would be worth doing.

> One of the reasons for doing the King's Fund is to show that you're committed to monitoring. There are lots of things that we do that are about reassuring patients about the type of care that they would receive.
>
> (Independent hospital)

The main concern of the private hospitals is that the King's Fund scheme is designed for large hospitals and the needs of the smaller hospitals were different. For this reason the HAP system had an appeal, designed as it is for small community hospitals. The small size of the independent hospitals may well have contributed to the ease with which any of the accreditation systems appeared to be accepted.

> We have only 500 staff so it is relatively easy to get them together to talk about changes.
>
> (Independent hospital)

Even so, the requirements of accreditation did seem to go against the culture of the independents, although most managers saw this as an advantage rather than a difficulty.

> Our staff were intimidated by the volume of the documentation required. We tended to do things in the past and never write them down.
>
> (Independent hospital)

There are differences between the private and the public sectors of health care which do suggest that a national system of standards will be unable to meet all internal quality assurance needs. For example, many of the King's Fund standards did not apply, and there were none to cover billing and the other differences in the financial systems.

> Medical records, libraries, outpatients, waiting times are not relevant to us. We would have preferred a section on business office accounting, billing etc.
>
> (Independent hospital)

> The King's Fund essentially breaks down into an NHS structure, and therefore there are sections of the audit that are not applicable to us so we'd be adapting and making do.
>
> (Independent hospital)

In addition, the King's Fund system does not accept the difference in orientation caused by the fact that the independent hospitals have a looser relationship with their clinicians.

> There are particular problems in private hospitals because clinicians do not want to do clinical audit. The surveyors expect there to be documentation on clinical standards and they expect to meet and talk to the clinicians.
>
> (Independent hospital)

> We do have problems in the private sector because medical records are very variable. Doctors take the view that they write up their clinical notes in their own format and we are still trying to find a way around that. If we upset the doctors too much they won't practice here and go elsewhere and we won't have a business.
>
> (Independent hospital)

Standards developed to meet the needs of independent hospitals might be useful in helping to achieve internal quality objectives, but by definition these would not enable comparability with the NHS. In addition, the independent sector is concerned about protecting its standards with regard to the practices of the NHS. This is particularly true of their need to control the work of clinicians within the private sector. Their perspective derives from the perceived lack of control over the work of the consultants.

> When people go to private hospitals, they assume that they'll get better care, but do they know if the consultant's any good? In general, we in the private sector, have to accept the consultant is competent. Ideally we would want to look at it and say, we've got two consultants, one has a high waiting list, they've got to get it down and we would start demanding that they do. Our job as managers is to provide the resources and the support to the consultant to achieve that objective.
>
> (Independent hospital)

The managers of the independent hospitals were unclear as to where accreditation would go in the future. They perceived a need for some form of regulation to control the activities of the health care market. Equally, they were also aware of the changing nature of medical care which called for different monitoring approaches. Many were convinced that there was a need to develop a greater clinical orientation in monitoring and therefore, if it were to happen, this would have to be included in the accreditation process.

> It is a bit like having your car serviced. Getting an MOT certificate and changing the oil is the King's Fund, and dealing with the trip computer is clinical audit.
>
> (Independent hospital)

The private sector is becoming increasingly interested in the idea of accreditation, both to improve standards within its own sector, and to improve its chances of competing with the NHS. There are a number of different pressures arising from the interest in accreditation which have the potential to pull the independent sector in different directions. The insurance companies have their own interests, notably to control provider entry into their insurance market. An accreditation system which 'grades' providers enables insurance companies to discriminate simply and easily between providers. The providers are concerned equally to remove adverse publicity and beliefs that may exist in the minds of the public and politicians about poor quality care in the private sector. If accreditation results in improved standards of care, across the board it will be beneficial. Or, if accreditation merely lays the ghost of perceived, rather than real, variability in quality, it will have achieved a useful objective. Finally, accreditation, if applied equally to public and private hospitals alike, will enable NHS purchasers to make cost/quality trade-offs between private and public sector care.

There are significant problems in creating an accreditation system which would meet these objectives. Private sector hospitals do not do the same work as public sector hospitals – frequently like is not being compared with like. There are issues about professional practices, about clinical attitudes, and about the general management of small scale institutions versus large scale ones. Even so, there is a recognition of the need for something approximating to accreditation. The issue is whether it is contained within the independent sector, or whether, on grounds of equity, for both the public receiving services and the hospitals competing with one another, accreditation should cover both the private and the public sectors.

From the participants' perspective, accreditation reflects its original purpose of helping managers to develop their organizations. It is directed at processes not at outcomes. As such, it operates as a tool of management. It reduces the administrative aspects of management to a set of standards which when complied with give a reassurance of minimal levels of quality. It is therefore a political rather than a scientific tool. As the larger acute units are finding in the UK, the accreditation exercise needs to carry weight, to support conviction both within and outside the organization. Without a grading, it carries no message to communicate simply how well the organization is doing. With a grading are problems in motivating staff when failure to succeed is perceived, or explaining to purchasers what has gone wrong. The whole emphasis of accreditation, however, depends upon the standards which are selected to form the basis for the exercise. And as the next chapter shows, there are many options available.

PART II

ISSUES IN THE DESIGN AND IMPLEMENTATION OF ACCREDITATION SYSTEMS

4

STANDARDS – DESIGN AND MEASUREMENT

Every accreditation system employs a system or process for measuring the organization or the service against selected standards. This process involves: determination of the standards; the processes for assessing compliance with the standards; the processes (if used) for 'scoring' performance or ranking it against others. There are many different ways in which each of these components can be implemented which will affect the nature and functioning of the accreditation process.

STANDARDS

In 1993 Elma Heidemann, Executive Director of the CCHFA reviewed the use of standards in health care on behalf of the World Health Organization. This review was conducted against the background that many countries are reviewing their current systems of health care delivery and seeking to modify them. Inevitably questions are raised as to whether hospitals are doing what they should be doing and whether they are doing it in an acceptable way. The report draws the conclusion that without standards there is no means of assessing either of these things. The report highlights three different aspects of standards which are key in understanding the relevance and the development of accreditation systems: the level, the type and the focus or scope of the standards.

LEVEL FOR STANDARDS

The level at which standards are set is the subject of considerable debate. Standards could be seen as the minimum with which a

Table 4.1   Canadian Council on Health Facilities Accreditation (1994: ACUTE-BETA 11–IM): standards for information management

Information systems are managed to facilitate clinical and managerial decision making throughout the facility. The team managing information at the corporate level assumes a coordinating role and provides support to their clients at all levels of the organization for the implementation of related processes.

1   There are processes for developing partnerships among those managing information at the corporate level.

1.1 There is a team approach to the management of information at the corporate level.

- evidence of team work is seen in:
  - interprofessional, functional and cross-functional involvement
  - planning, implementing and quality monitoring
  - decision making, problem solving and priority setting
  - resource allocation

Rating
1 = comprehensive   2 = coordinated   3 = client centred
4 = communicated   5 = collaborative

Score
N = non-compliance   M = minimal compliance   P = partial compliance
S = substantial achievement

Source: Reprinted with permission from the proposed 1995 Standards for the Canadian Council on Health Facilities Accreditation.

community may be reasonably content. However, in professional terms minimum tends not to be an acceptable level of operation. Minima suggest levels below which any operation would be unacceptable. To a large extent this is the difference between regulation and accreditation. Minimum standards tend to be the basis on which rules and regulations operate. Over time, accreditation standards moved away from minima and have been cast in the language of professionals – representing degrees of excellence. Thus the stated goal of the CCHFA is 'to promote and encourage by voluntary means an optimal quality of health care in all its respects by the achievement of accreditation standards in all hospitals and related health organizations in the health care field' (Canadian Council on Health Facilities Accreditation 1992).

The Australian standards are described as reasonable, contemporary, professional, surveyable, consensus and optimal (Australian Council on Hospital Standards 1986). The Australian use of the word optimal is considered vague (Lloyd 1987; McAlary 1981) having something to do with the highest quantitative level. The Canadians have adopted a more workable definition, optimal standards within the confines of resource constraints: 'Optimal standards do not necessarily represent the theoretical maximum, but rather they depict the best possible level that can be achieved given the available resources (Canadian Council on Health Facilities Accreditation 1992).

But there is difficulty in determining the orientation of the standards. On the one hand, it is possible to envisage excellence without demonstrating its achievement. This presents aspirational targets to which services can strive. On the other hand it is argued that standards should reflect achievable levels of practice within the limits of available resources. As individual hospitals or health services find ways of improving service delivery, outstripping the existing standards, so a new level of care is shown to be possible. The standards are therefore capable of continuous upgrading.

TYPES OF STANDARD

There are different types of standard depending upon the aspects of health care to which they are directed. These are frequently described, *à la* Donabedian, as structure, process or outcome. Structure is concerned with resources, human, financial or physical; process with activity; and outcome with the results of actions. Standards have typically been concerned with structure and process. The WHO report attributes this to the prevailing belief in a system theoretic approach to service delivery, that is, if the resources were used appropriately and effectively then the outcome of care would be desirable.

The standards of the three Anglophone models and their UK derivatives are based, originally, upon the theory that good organization practices will create an appropriate environment in which professionals can practise. This will lead to the safeguarding of professional standards and ensure that patients are protected from the worst effects of poor health care environments and the detrimental effects that poor environments may have upon professional

Table 4.2   Australian Council on Healthcare Standards: standard for medical record contents

---

An accurate medical record is maintained to facilitate efficient and effective patient care, evaluation of the care provided, a retrieval of data for research and management.

Criteria

1 Each health professional is responsible for documentation of the clinical care given and the standard of that documentation.
2 A medical record committee or equivalent, which includes the person in charge of the medical records service, reports to management and will monitor the following:

   (a) standards and policies for medical records are determined having regard to AS.2828 'Hospital Medical Records' and according to the relevant state regulations and requirements.
   (b) the content of medical records is regularly analysed to ascertain that the recorded clinical information is sufficient for the purpose of providing and evaluating patient care and for retrieval of data for management information, research and medico-legal reference.
   (c) policy or procedural changes are initiated after considering multidisciplinary input from health personnel who contribute substantially to the medical record.

. . . continued

Source: Reprinted with permission from The ACHS Accreditation Guide Australian Council on Healthcare Standards, 1993.

practice. The theory assumes that professionals cannot work optimally unless appropriately organized, if using faulty equipment, if the organizational system functions inefficiently with lost notes, unhygienic practices or without adequate precautions to protect physical safety.

Over time the coverage of the standards widened but the emphasis remained on organizational practices. The hospital standards which have evolved for service areas in the four Anglophone countries are remarkably similar in content. They all reflect a common understanding of the nature of hospital care. There were, however, differences in the way in which the standards were ordered in the manuals, and some differences evolved in the focus of the standards, primarily because of different philosophies about hospital organization. The USA system, in which physicians are

Table 4.3 Joint Commission on Accreditation of Healthcare Organizations: standard IM.7 on patient specific data and information

The information-management function provides for the definition, capture, analysis, transformation, transmission, and reporting of individual patient-specific data and information related to the process(es) and/or the outcome of the patient's care.

IM.7.1	The organization initiates and maintains a medical record for every individual 1 2 3 4 5 assessed or treated. The medical record incorporates information from subsequent contacts between the patient and the organization.
IM.7.2	Entries in medical records are made only by individuals authorized to do so as specified in organizational and medical staff policies.

Source: Reprinted with permission from the 1995 Comprehensive Accreditation Manual for Hospitals. Copyright Joint Commission on Accreditation of Healthcare Organizations, Oakbrook Terrace, Illinois 60181 USA.

rarely employees of hospitals, developed a different approach to the handling of medical staff. The JCAHO standards also reflect a stronger orientation towards professional activities. Although it is impossible to make precise comparisons across the standards as each recognizes different aspects of the health care delivery process identified by the different countries, it is possible to detect the difference in tone between the systems (see Tables 4.2, 4.3, 4.4 and 4.5).

Although standards encompass the hotel services and structural fabric of the hospital, the majority address the activities of clinical departments. Hard experience has shown that the assumption that appropriately organized inputs lead to good outcomes is not proved (Hadley and McGuerrin 1988). There has therefore been a move, as we have seen, to define outcome standards. Each country's accreditation system faces exactly this problem and is now trying to decide whether outcome standards should complement structure and process standards or replace them. In addition there is the two sided problem of whether it is better to develop new and additional outcome standards thus increasing the total number of standards, or whether, in response to popular demand to reduce the number of standards to replace structure and process standards with outcome standards.

Table 4.4   King's Fund Organisational Audit: information services
standards

The hospital/trust collects, stores and uses accurate information which
enables informed decisions to be made.

Criteria	Weighting
7.1 There is a written management/technology strategy for the hospital/trust.	A
7.2 Information systems enable the minimum data standards to be met.	A

Interpretation

These information systems:
• identify the purchasing authority for each patient seen
• identify the registered GP for each patient
• assign contract numbers to each patient episode
• assign clinical codes at discharge or within 14 days using a current
  version of the international classification of diseases and OPCS4
  procedure codes
• group patients using a current grouping system

Weighting: A = essential practice   B = good practice
             C = desirable practice

Source: Reprinted with permission from the proposed 1995 Standards for the King's
Fund Organisational Audit Hospital Accreditation programme.

Table 4.5   Scoring scale/level of compliance for JCAHO

Score 1   **Substantial compliance**. The organization consistently meets all
major provisions of the standard.

Score 2   **Significant compliance**. The organization meets most of the
provisions of the standard.

Score 3   **Partial compliance**. The organization meets some provisions of
the standard.

Score 4   **Minimal compliance**. The organization meets few provisions of
the standard.

Score 5   **Non-compliance**. The organization fails to meet the provisions of
the standard.

Source: Reprinted with permission from the 1995 Comprehensive Accreditation
Manual for Hospitals. Copyright Joint Commission on Accreditation of Healthcare
Organizations, Oakbrook Terrace, Illinois 60181 USA.

This is not a simple issue. On the one hand, outcome standards may demonstrate how well a hospital is contributing to patient health and well being. But it is not clear that the hospital is being well run as an organization. And this raises two separate but related issues. It may be that good organization does underpin good clinical care and failure to deliver adequate outcomes can be traced back to poor internal structures and processes. But equally it may be that there are definitions of the appropriate acceptable functioning of the internal management of a hospital which although they do not necessarily contribute directly to patient outcomes, none the less for reasons of public accountability should be enshrined in standards. The JCAHO is addressing the problems of dealing with three different types of standards and is discovering that not all are compatible (Clarke and O'Leary 1987). It would appear that the direction or focus of any accreditation system therefore has to be clearly specified if coherence in the standards is to be maintained.

In the 'Agenda for Change' (see Chapter 1) the JCAHO (1993) has embraced the paradigm of continuous quality improvement. The intention is to move accreditation from asking 'has the hospital the capability for producing quality care?' to asking 'does the hospital provide quality care?' There are two elements in this new strategy. The first has been to put increasing emphasis on the processes whereby the hospital itself reviews the quality of care being provided: increasingly the role of the surveyors is to monitor the way in which the hospitals themselves assess the quality of clinical services being delivered. The second, now being implemented, is to move from defining quality in terms of inputs (physical plant; organizational structure) and processes (policies and plans for the delivery of care) to outcomes: a move which reflects scepticism about whether there is any relationship between inputs and processes, on the one hand and outcomes on the other hand.

Accordingly the JCAHO has embarked on an ambitious and expensive programme for developing clinical indicators which reflect hospital outcomes. This has built upon the work of an earlier voluntary programme (developed by the Commission of Professional and Hospital Activities) which provided comparative statistics for hospitals which volunteered to supply data to the programme. Concurrently, the JCAHO is engaged in reducing and simplifying the input and process standards required: its 1994 *Accreditation Manual for Hospitals* marks a significant step in this direction, reversing the trend towards ever increasing complexity of previous decades. The 1994 Manual also signalled a move away from defining standards in terms of specific services or departments and adopting a more cross-cutting, thematic approach, testing the functioning of the hospital as a whole by examining such issues as the way in which medication is handled or the problem of avoiding infections is handled. The JCAHO has not been alone in this revision of its approach. The US Department of Health and Human Services has moved its standards for Medicare and Medicaid in the same direction.

The idea is that clinical indicators will be used to flag up areas where there are potential problems in the delivery of health care. This approach is also being adopted by the ACHS (LoGerfo 1990). The Australian approach is to suggest that advice should be sought from the relevant clinical colleges. The data examined by the accreditation body will remain confidential to the hospital under review. But the end product should be greater involvement of the clinical colleges in the accreditation process. These are steps towards the development of performance indicators which will enable comparisons between hospitals to take place. In this case accreditation is moving more towards an audit model in which the practices of organizations are reviewed so that problem areas can be identified and addressed. This will enable the accreditors to home in on particular areas rather than adopting the holistic approach of the past.

The JCAHO has defined clinical indicators as 'a quantitative measure which can be used as a guide to monitor and evaluate the quality of important patient care and support service activities' (Quality Review Bulletin 1989). The indicators focus on patient care, and also focus upon the integration of services and the collaboration of professionals in providing care. The shift has therefore been away from efficiency towards effectiveness based upon a particular definition of quality of patient care. Quality is seen as being determined by a number of dimensions of the patient care process. Accessability, timeliness, effectiveness, efficacy, appropriateness, efficiency, continuity, privacy and confidentiality, participation of the patient and patient family, and safety and supportiveness of the care environment.'

The clinical indicators are of two types: outcome (which measures what happens) or process (which measures the care provided to a patient). These can also be of two types: sentinel events which measure serious and often avoidable outcomes (deaths or damage to patients fall into this category); and rate-based events which measure certain aspects of patient care for which a certain rate of occurrence is acceptable. In this way, an organization can assess its progress over time or in comparison with others.

An example of an outcome indicator (provided in Quality Review Bulletin 1989) might be the number of patients who fail to emerge from general anaesthesia within one hour of termination of anaesthesia relative to the number of patients who receive general anaesthesia. A process indicator might be the number of Caesarean sections performed on certain days of the week. Where there is unexplained variation, it would be possible to question the hospital's practices in this area. The performance measurement framework of clinical performance looks at prevention, early detection, appropriateness of care and effectiveness of care, patient satisfaction and health status. They have also identified priorities for clinical performance measures in obstetrics, anaesthetics, cardiovascular disease, oncology, trauma and mental health.

The JCAHO system is intended to become part of a national reference database into which hospitals will submit quarterly data. However, the USA system differs from the Australian one in that its purpose is to provide national comparative information. And unlike Australia, the JCAHO is unclear as to how this will fit into the accreditation process. The JCAHO has claimed that it favours making participation in the indicator exercise mandatory. In order to get enough data to make national comparisons possible, any data collection system requires one hundred per cent participation. Opposition to this move was encountered early on in its development. Resistance came from those who believe that they are already collecting quality indicators for state organizations. And it had begun to move into a market which existing participants felt was providing them with an unfair competitive advantage. And all health services (as equally, the UK experience described in the previous chapter shows) have never found data collection an easy task, and in general prefer to avoid the time consuming the frequently expensive task (Bergman 1993a).

If the way forward is the collection of such indicators, then the whole virtue of accreditation becomes questionable. Mandatory data collection is a long way from voluntary participation. The analysis of current activity is an equally long way from aspirational standards and the professional striving to improve practice. This activity may well be better undertaken by a government body, or a government associated body rather than an accreditation body. We will return to this point later.

FOCUS OR SCOPE OF STANDARDS

The standards of accreditation systems tend to focus on either the organization and management of health care or on clinical practice: 'Organization and management standards tend to address the ability of the health care facility to deliver quality care or service. Clinical practice standards on the other hand, describe the precise nature of what should be delivered' (Heidemann 1993: 7). Heidemann claims that there is a place for both sorts of standards in assessing the quality of health care provided. However, trying to develop both sets of standards to operate in a cooperative, rather than conflicting manner presents fundamental problems.

In the United States the hospitals which have not volunteered for accreditation tend to be those which are small and rural and which claim that they cannot afford to go through the programme. It is curious therefore that within the National Health Service three systems (HAP, Trent and now the King's Fund) have evolved in community hospitals. Is this just coincidence, or is there something about UK community hospitals which lend themselves to the processes of accreditation more readily than the other services? In contrast, the ACHS and the JCAHO have both been determined that standards must be applicable to all hospitals, no matter what their size. Yet Canada and the UK have developed different systems for different sized hospitals. This may be culturally determined, in that the UK certainly has always treated small hospitals as a very different phenomenon from the large acute hospitals. Indeed, different policy cycles have demanded the closure of small hospitals on the grounds of either inefficiency or as being clinically unsound. In the climate of GP fundholding, the small hospitals have returned to favour being the province of general practitioners. Certainly this may explain the difference in attitude in the UK. The small hospitals perform different functions from the larger ones, being restricted to convalescing patients or very limited surgical operations. Their work is therefore rarely compared with that of the larger organizations.

The JCAHO and the CCHFA have both revised their standards to reflect the changing emphasis of health care on the patient experience. The JCAHO standards have been redesigned to encompass eight aspects of patient care: patients' rights, admission to the service setting, patient evaluation, nutritional care, non-operative treatment and administration, operative and other invasive procedures, patient and family education, and continuity of care. These have been classified into three sections within the manual (1995): patient-focused functions, organizational functions and structures with functions. In 1994 the scope of the Canadian standards related to government policy, a second set of standards relating to the management of the organization and a third set relating to hospital or health service departments. Within these the standards relate to three main questions: first, where are you going as a department or service, which covers planning and the departmental mission? Second, how do you get there in terms of staffing, resources and competencies? Third, what is the result of what you do in terms of quality assessment and quality assurance? The second set of standards, relating to human resources, examine hiring policies, performance review and competencies. There are also standards which look at environmental management, hotel services, risk management for safety, infection control etc.

In 1995 the Canadians will move towards a set of standards based on a quality improvement philosophy away from departmental divisions towards the major functions of the organization. The standards in the future will address the care of the patient or client from the time of admission to patient follow-up. These standards are intended to address admission, needs assessment, planning, treatment and evaluation of care. The manual will be divided into six major sections: individual patient care groups that correspond to particular episodes of care; clinical partnerships; information management; human resources development and management; environmental management; and leadership and partnerships. The surveyors will talk to a team of professionals who will be questioned on how the patient moves from admission to discharge.

The relationships within health care are also changing, as the boundaries of primary and secondary care change. The JCAHO approach to accrediting networks has required them to acknowledge the existence of other accreditation systems. Compliance with standards is required for the network as a whole, for the component organizations and for the practitioner sites across the network. From 1997 there will be additional indicators for clinical performance which will be applied across all the different organizations contributing to the network. But the JCAHO has allowed accreditation from other bodies which accredit within the health care system to be taken into account in their award of accreditation status.

This is a significant development. It offers one solution to the problem encountered by all accreditation systems which are trying to reflect the new structures of the health service. The JCAHO has demonstrated that it is possible to accredit services which cut across organizations, it is possible to accredit what are effectively purchasing organizations, and furthermore, it is possible to bring together a number of competing accreditation systems within a single accreditation framework.

SCALING AND SCORING

A single number which describes how well an organization is performing has been considered desirable in health care for many years. Accreditation offers this in its scaled grading score. However, accreditation has tended to be applied to whole institutions, summing the activities of a range of different departments. Therefore, the final score is subject to the problems of aggregation faced by any multivariate scoring system. Each standard must contribute to the overall score. A bad score in one area will negate a good score in another. One poorly performing department could result in a poor overall score. This presents problems not only for the interpretation of the scoring, but also the judgements of individual surveyors which are required to assign the score in the first place. On the other hand, as discussed above, the JCAHO has been criticized for not failing unsatisfactory hospitals. Yet in 1987 to 1989 it published findings that more than two-thirds of all hospitals were unable to satisfactorily demonstrate that they managed the quality and safety of the patient care physical environment. According to Health Care Financing Administration (HCFA) these were enough to fail hospitals, but the JCAHO differed with this assessment (Koska 1992a).

One view is that standards and the criteria to judge them should be framed in such a way that a lay person could administer them and judge whether a hospital complies. In this way standards' assessment strives for objectivity. An alternative view is that standards are by definition merely tools to assist professional judgement, and therefore standards should be interpreted flexibly by surveyors, who must have enough knowledge themselves of the subject under review to be able to make such interpretations. No accreditation system has found a satisfactory answer to this particular conundrum. The USA system uses a small number of full-time surveyors to supplement their part-time, often retired, and clinically active volunteer force. The full-time and retired surveyors, by definition must be following the former model. No matter how much professional experience they have had in the past, they will not be practitioners in their field when they are full-time surveyors. Their judgements must therefore be based upon some independent criteria. Australia and Canada use practitioners, who may be steeped in professional practice, but may not be knowledgeable about the scope of good practice within a complete hospital (see Chapter 5).

STANDARDS AND ASSESSMENT CRITERIA

Underpinning any discussion of the application of standards is a concern about how well standards are met. There are two different approaches to the construction of standards. One is to write detailed statements which are each standards in their own right. The other is to devise more general standards and to assign assessment criteria which enable the judgement of compliance to be made. It is in this, that perhaps the greatest differences occur between the accreditation systems. The JCAHO has evolved very detailed and specific standards. The Australians (and the King's Fund following their lead) in contrast have very general standards with specific criteria to assess the extent of compliance.

There are many different ways of scoring compliance with standards. The JCAHO employs a five point score, with one demonstrating excellence, and five demonstrating poor or no compliance (see Table 4.5). The Canadian system is moving towards a three stage process. The proposed process starts with assessing compliance for an individual standard; then compliance is assessed for a standards area and section; finally compliance is assessed for the whole organization. In the first stage, the existence of the process is ascertained. If the process does not exist, a rating of non-compliance or non-applicable is made for the standard. If the process is in place, a decision must be made about the level of compliance. This is a two dimensional score. The rating can be: minimal, partial or substantial (see Table 4.6) and is applied to three elements: completeness, communication and coordination, and client/patient focus. The element of completeness examines the extent to which the standard is being met. Communication and coordination looks at whether the information about the process is being shared with all appropriate individuals and groups for example, clients, patients, staff and suppliers. The client/patient focus

Table 4.6   Levels of compliance for CCHFA

N   Non-applicable or non-compliant. Used when a standard does not apply or when the requirements of the standard are not met.

M   Minimal compliance used when few provisions of the standard and related criteria are met and also when ineffective communication and coordination of the process results in significant gaps in implementation of the process.

P   Partial compliance used when most provisions of the standard and related criteria are met.

S   Substantial compliance used when all provisions of the standard and related criteria are consistently met.

Source: Reprinted with permission from the Canadian Council on Health Facilities Accreditation – Standards for Acute Care for 1995.

concentrates on the extent to which the mechanisms provide for client input and feedback, and how this information is being used in improving processes. In the second stage, the ratings for the individual standards are combined to provide a single rating for each standards area. And finally, the surveyors have to determine the organization's overall compliance level, which then determines the award level which the surveyors recommend to the CCHFA. This is followed by a further assessment which examines quality monitoring activities. The assessment is completed for each major section of the standards and examines three elements of quality monitoring. First, establishing indicators of quality; second, monitoring performance against indicators; third, utilising findings to make improvements. The facility is then rated according to how well it complies with these various components.

The Australian system uses a similar scoring system compliance with individual standards (see Table 4.7) again using criteria to assess compliance. The King's Fund has the most simplistic scoring system of yes or no scoring.

From these different approaches there have evolved different ways of building the overall score for a health care facility. The JCAHO has evolved a complex system of checks and balances. The results from the surveyors are checked by teams of trained staff for consistency and accuracy. Scores derived from the assessment of compliance are aggregated into a decision grid which is then analysed using complex decision algorithms which enable a final score to be calculated. None of the other systems have evolved such

Table 4.7   Compliance code for the Australian Council on Healthcare Standards

---

SC Substantial compliance
SC does not necessarily denote total compliance and on occasions it may be considered necessary by the surveyor to make a recommendation where this would significantly affect the facility.

PC Partial compliance
PC means that there is a substantial part of the criterion which, in the opinion of the surveyor, does not comply with the standard.

NC Non-compliance
used when the facility does not comply with the standard.

NA Not applicable

Source: Reproduced with permission of the Australian Council on Healthcare Standards.

a complex procedure to justify their decisions. This can be explained as part of the cultural approach of the USA. It is likely to be due to the two obvious differences between the United States and other health care systems which accreditation operates. First, that the final grading has become part of the process for allocating public funds and has therefore created a highly defensive attitude on the part of surveyed organizations. Second, that many US hospitals operate (and compete) in a market. A hospital may require a successful review from the JCAHO in order to obtain not only its Medicare and Medicaid funding allocations, but also to treat patients from the major insurance companies. Without it, the result would be financially disastrous.

In contrast the King's Fund is evolving a weighted approach which will lead to three types of standards. The first are those designated as essential practice. Failure to achieve them will compromise the safety of staff and patients. Staff, patients or visitors will be at risk (that is on the ground of health, safety, or legal liability). Patients' rights or statutory requirements will not be met. The second category includes good practice. The third is desirable practice which is the means of advancing or improving practice.

To apply the standards and the criteria requires independent judgements. Who makes the judgements, which criteria are selected and how these are applied are all variables which any accreditation system needs to address. The JCAHO has sought to ensure consistency in the application of the methods of assessment. This is an important dimension of an accreditation system which has moved into the external review model and which has a number of audiences for its gradings. Hospitals can lose income or be closed down if they fail to achieve the necessary grade. In the less harsh environments of Canada and Australia, the criteria are fuzzier and more open to individual discussion and interpretation. Judgements are made by peers whose additional role is to make observations which can assist in organizational development. In these systems the public interest is still, for the time being, in whether a hospital is prepared to participate in the accreditation programme, rather than specifically in the judgements made by the surveyors and the accrediting bodies. The motivational orientation of review by peers is held to encourage staff to strive for excellence rather than to guarantee standards. But, the move to a model which responds to external pressures has created a degree of confusion about the interpretation of the findings of the accreditation process.

The tension between public accountability and professional accountability is a characteristic of all accreditation systems. With the exception of the King's Fund, all of the systems can defer or refuse accreditation status to participants who fail to meet the required standards. This suggests that although they are all publicly committed to the notion of optimal achievable standards, they enforce minimal levels below which health care organizations should not function.

DEVELOPING STANDARDS

The JCAHO has an impressive system for establishing consensus over its standards. New standards are sent out to hospitals to try them, they are then tested for surveyability, and then they are monitored for scoring. High levels of non-compliance result in a standard being abandoned. There is little point in having a standard which is too far ahead of current practice. Standards which are considered to be too expensive or of little relevance to hospitals are not useful either. This consensus approach follows the principles of the market. There is no point in trying to sell something people do not want nor have little use for. The JCAHO is very aware that participating hospitals and health services are its customers.

The Canadians have developed an equally significant although different approach, more in a democratic, participative model. All participants in the scheme have the right to be consulted over any changes in the standards or procedures. Extensive consultation is also carried out with all of the professional bodies who may be affected by accreditation.

The different approaches reflect the very different cultural and national environments in which the two systems operate. The JCAHO has a legal relationship with the licensing bodies of 42 of its states but there is no requirement for hospitals to participate. The CCHFA has no formal relationship with its government at all, but there is a legal requirement for a national approach to health care, and comparability of provision across the ten independent provinces.

Such approaches have proved successful where the main body of standards has already been developed, or when there is a readily accessible constituency from whom advice and opinions can be obtained. Greater difficulty is experienced where standards have to be constructed from 'scratch'. The United Kingdom bodies which have been attempting to develop new and different approaches to service delivery with either no, or very small constituencies have had to find alternative ways of developing standards. The King's Fund for example, approached the complex area of developing standards for primary care by involving working groups and organizational sites in which the standards were piloted. Each pilot site established a multidisciplinary group, responsible for coordinating the various stages of the project. Two representatives from each health centre or general practice were selected to join a central working group. And to provide further advice, a national advisory group was established, using representatives from professional and consumer organizations which have an interest and expertise in primary care to provide independent advice. Each of the pilot sites focused upon one or two of the areas identified. Members of the local steering group assigned to the pilot sites developed standards in consultation with colleagues and consumer groups. The standards were then collated by the King's Fund and circulated to the pilot sites for comment by both staff and consumers. These comments and views were then put to the central working group and national advisory group. Again the emphasis was upon producing a consensus between the involved parties on the standards which were then piloted.

The approach adopted by the former South East Thames Regional Health Authority in the United Kingdom has been similar. A working group, made up of a variety of people working in primary care, from different professional backgrounds examined existing

Table 4.8 Guiding principles for primary health care for the King's Fund Organisational Audit

---

- Support the patient's/client's expectations of quality care and personal dignity
- Be desirable and measurable
- Relate as directly as possible to the quality of care and the quality of the environment in which care is provided
- Emphasize an efficient and effective use of available resources
- Represent a consensus on currently accepted professional practice
- State objectives rather than mechanisms for meeting objectives

---

Source: Reprinted with permission from the 1994 Primary Health Care Organisational Standards and Criteria.

systems of audit and quality assurance, inviting contributions from outside experts. The result was a set of standards which define and describe good practice. These have then been produced as a template against which practices can measure themselves.

Comparison of the two approaches reveals the subtle differences in the approach adopted by the two organizations. Although the King's Fund did not start with its own standards, it had an approach inherited from Australia and adapted for the UK NHS. South East Thames started from its own assessment of good practice, long before it had begun to consider the approach to accreditation. The ensuing principles from the King's Fund reflect the commitment to good organization (see for example, Table 4.8). The South East Thames are cast in more professional terms, describing their relationship, and the patient's relationship to the service (see Table 4.9).

The JCAHO operates six general principles in the development of standards. Standards should focus on quality of care and the environment only. They must be achievable, that is, they must be within the current state of the art. The standards must be surveyable, that is, there must be a measurable and tangible way of demonstrating compliance. Finally the standards are reviewed every year for hospitals and every two years for other types of organization.

The rate of revision is significant. The CCHFA reviews its standards every two years not annually. Other accreditation systems rarely change their standards unless they are found to be very outdated. To some extent this must depend upon the size of the organization which supports the accreditation system. Many of the

Table 4.9   Principles for primary health care for South East Thames Regional Health Authority

---

A first class service that delivers excellence

The residents of the region should be able to expect excellence from their general practice.

Services should be shaped to promote health and well-being as well as providing diagnosis, referral and treatment for illness, disability and long-term infirmity.

Primary health care services which reflect the needs of individuals and the local population and the ability of the primary health care team to meet them should be provided locally.

General practice should refer patients to acute, community and social providers to provide the full range of diagnostic, investigative treatment, care and support services as required.

General practice will play a full part in needs assessment and care management procedures for individual patients where required, meeting its obligations under community care legislation and the Children Act.

A service which puts the patient first

All individuals have the right to be registered with a general practitioner.

Patients should be treated with due regard to individual dignity, privacy and respect.

The cultural and personal beliefs of the patient will be respected at all times and services shaped to the value and the contributions of differing cultures to the care process.

The services of a general practitioner shall be available to all individuals whatever their special needs may be.

Patients and, where appropriate, the relatives, friends and significant others (always with the patient's consent), will be kept informed of clinical progress and prognosis.

Individuals will be informed and given advice about difficult options, patterns of treatment and the consequences (including financial aspects) of their care.

Where the consent of an individual is required for treatment or the participation in research or for teaching purposes, he or she will be given the choice of whether to participate and the potential risks and benefits will be clearly explained. Individuals will be assured that refusal to participate will not jeopardize their care or treatment.

continued

Table 4.9 Continued

An expert service that is part of general NIS provision

Patients are entitled to have access to services equipped to care for any conditions which require specialist advice, treatment and care.

Services should be tailored, along with those provided by acute, community and social care providers, to ensure continuity of care for the patient.

Multiprofessional audit should be developed to monitor, review and improve the quality, effectiveness and efficiency of treatment and care, and to test the satisfaction of patients and their carers.

Excellent communication between all those providing care should be the cornerstone of promptly delivered, appropriate and well-managed services.

The primary health care team will work alongside and together with specialist services to provide continuing care of patients with particular needs (for example terminally ill patients).

The acquisition of relevant and up-to-date skills and continuing education should be seen as prerequisites for the efficient functioning of the primary health care team.

Source: Reprinted with permission from the 1994 standards of the Directorate of Nursing, Quality and Programmes, South East Thames Regional Health Authority.

smaller accrediting bodies do not have the personnel or the re-sources to review standards which can therefore fall into disrepute or irrelevance. The UK system has a number of accreditation bodies which are too small to sustain the continual revision of standards and therefore they have a difficult task in competing with other means and methods of promoting quality.

The JCAHO standards do contain normative elements which are interpreted by professionals as changes in requirements for good practice. For example, the changes in nursing standards introduced in 1991 can be interpreted as changing the role and activities of nursing. Under the old standards it was not clear who had responsi-bility for planning patient care. Under the new standards authority is clearly delegated to a nurse executive (Hurley 1991). To stay ahead of current practice standards need to be continually refined and rewritten and to some extent they must by definition create good practice as well as reflect it. The JCAHO has also developed new standards to cover new areas such as information management.

In this, the standards demand integrated information systems. Although this may be seen as good practice, it is a problem for hospitals which have failed to develop integrated systems or which have chosen deliberately not to do so. The standards demand that they try and succeed. Here, in an area which is so difficult to implement, it is interesting that an external agency should try to force the pace of change. It may well be that an independent agency can encourage such steps to be taken, whereas government departments may find themselves faced with considerable criticism and demands for extra resources.

Some standards require changes in the behaviour of practitioners. Others require changes in policies and procedures and systems to support their implementation. In a number of cases, immediate achievement of the standards may not be possible. Staff may need time to understand the standards, and to find ways of complying with them (Longo *et al.* 1986). In 1985, the JCAHO introduced an approach called implementation monitoring which allows accredited organizations time to gain experience of and implement designated standards, without putting their accreditation status at risk.

The experience of the JCAHO suggests that hospitals find greater difficulty in dealing with standards which relate to new services, especially those relating to quality assurance – with which the institution is unfamiliar (Longo *et al.* 1986). As hospitals began to move into ambulatory care, a large number were found to be having difficulty achieving standards regarding the monitoring and evaluation of the new services. And a perennial problem for hospitals has been quality assurance involving medical staff who were reluctant to become involved in quality initiatives.

The choice of standards is not something that can be done in isolation. The selection depends upon the perceived purpose of the accreditation system and its focus, as well as reflecting assumptions about the relationship between the inputs and the outcomes of the health care system. Accreditation may be perceived as offering self-reassurance for an institution, enabling it to demonstrate that it is working at acceptable levels. On the other hand, accreditation may be interpreted as offering a means of signalling to the outside world that standards are being achieved. It does this primarily by offering a grading of the institution. For some, the existence of the programme may be enough to ensure accountability. Purchasers and the public may wish to see that the hospital is prepared to enter into such a programme as a gesture of good intentions. There is limited evidence that accreditation motivates providers to maintain or improve their quality of care (Hadley and McGuerrin 1988). In this particular case the rated outcome is not necessary. But, it can be argued that if a system exists which is capable of providing comparative measures of success (compliance with standards), the measures themselves may become the most important aspect of the process. And like any measures, it is possible to view these as individual ratings, or as scalings against which individual hospitals can be compared.

There is another, associated conundrum in any system which is designed to measure compliance with standards. Where there is lack of consensus on policy, the standard can only reflect administrative intention. So, traditionally standards have asked for evidence of the existence of policies, and not been directed at the content of policies. The greater the specificity of the standards, the more likely the standard is to be setting policy.

'Formal standards adopted by authoritative external control agencies not only embody policy, they are policy' (Vladeck 1988). The design of standards therefore can generate some interesting issues. If standards are made too explicit, they will in fact be writing policies which may have some difficult professional and potentially legal consequences. For example, a standard which says that a trauma department (accident and emergency) should have a policy for dealing with head injuries is operating at one level of prescription. But it is possible to argue that simply having a policy is not adequate protection of the patient. The staff must demonstrate that they know about the policy. And professionals involved in this work may have a very different view about the correctness or appropriateness of the policy. Where should the design of the standard stop in the level of specificity? In the last case, the standard incorporates professional policy and therefore is on the one hand, controlling professional practice, and on the other hand is leaving the accreditation body open to criticism for adopting an approach on which there is undoubtedly no professional consensus. The boundaries of professional behaviour are very sensitive. A standard which for example does more than suggest that professional behaviour is to be conducted in an acceptable fashion will run into problems.

Standards are only half of the accreditation picture. A complete organization is required if assessment of compliance is to be undertaken. The next chapter examines the issues facing accrediting bodies in determining their internal structure and functioning.

5

THE ORGANIZATION OF ACCREDITATION SYSTEMS

Every accreditation system requires an organizational structure: not only to administer its activities, but also to develop standards, and organize and control the work of surveyors. This necessitates constitutions to control the activities of the organization, and internal policies and procedures for how their business will be conducted.

CORPORATE GOVERNANCE

Accreditation, in theory, should be an independent objective process, highly credible, unbiased, and should represent the widest possible consensus. For many organizations the main method of achieving consensus is through representation on the governing body or board. The board of an accreditation system contains representatives of professional organizations. Like most bodies which require professional support, it has proved necessary to have representatives from the relevant interested organizations. As the scope of accreditation has widened, there has been a greater need for representation which has resulted in greater board membership.

The composition of the board is crucial to the acceptability of the accreditation system to the various components of the health care system, particularly the professional bodies without whose cooperation accreditation is a worthless exercise. The main issue faced by any accreditation scheme is the need to ensure that the professionals will accept the findings of the board and act upon their recommendations. The very existence of standards which can be reviewed by lay people, no matter how well trained, threatens the whole paradigm of professionalization. The viability of the

accreditation system therefore depends upon professional cooperation, and the best accepted way of dealing with this is to invite
representatives to join the board. The difficulty encountered by all
has been the rapid expansion of professional bodies within the
health care field. If all groups are represented, the board would be
too large to be manageable.

The CCHFA has attempted to expand the participation of interested groups in its activities by establishing a broad consultation
process. Approximately 100 professional bodies are consulted in
two ways: first, individually regarding specific standards and
second, at twice yearly meetings to which all participants are invited
to be briefed on the Council activities. Recent legislation passed in
Australia requires that board members or any organization have to
act in the interest of the organization of the board, rather than the
organization they might represent. Board members are therefore
required to act in the interests of the ACHS. This potentially
threatens the traditional concept of professional representation on
such bodies. If this becomes an international trend, the constitution
of multidisciplinary regulatory bodies will be brought into question
world-wide.

All the boards are trying to find ways of adapting to meet the
demands for including adequate consumer representation in their
work. The JCAHO has a number of public members, company
directors, an ethicist and a priest. The other boards are following a
similar route to incorporate consumers to add another dimension to
the board decision making. This follows a general trend in health
care to become more responsive to the needs and wishes of consumers. Driven by popular trends towards empowering consumers,
the accreditation systems are forced to respond by altering their
constitution. But this potentially creates an imbalance in the operations of the board. Non-professionals may bring either business
acumen or other forms of personal experience. But these are not
representatives of the patient at large. Representatives from consumer organizations may bring perspectives which reflect the views
of their parent bodies. But none can truly represent the views of
individual patients who have no body equivalent to the professional
bodies which dictate the limits of acceptable behaviour.

The shift in emphasis from a professional to a consumer orientation may be necessary but brings with it some very complex issues
of public accountability. The accreditation bodies have perceived a
duty to move their standards to reflect a patient or consumer
perspective which affects the orientation of the service delivery

processes. But they now face growing pressures to break the professional/client relationship they have with their customer organizations. More and more people, including consumers, are demanding the right to know the outcome of the survey visits and the assessments which are made.

THE RELATIONSHIP WITH THEIR CUSTOMERS

The accreditation systems are all run as self-funding, independent businesses, charging fees for participation in their processes. All therefore face the traditional marketing problems of meeting their customers' needs, but they face the additional problems of responding to broader issues of professional interests. In the earlier discussion, the educational component of accreditation has been raised many times. Although this is presented by the accrediting bodies as an integral part of the accreditation purpose, it also serves to provide an extra dimension – that of 'added value'. Participating organizations need to feel that they are getting value for money for taking part in the process. If they do not, they may begin to question the value of accreditation. To this end, the accrediting bodies have had to adapt to meet market needs and make decisions about how to develop and adapt their products.

Both the UK systems emphasize the benefits of pre-survey scrutiny and preparation. But neither of these, nor the JCAHO nor the ACHS require pre-assessment as a part of the accreditation process. In contrast, the Canadian survey process is divided into two discrete parts. First, self-assessment, in which each organization reviews itself against the standards and forms its own judgement of how well it is doing. Second is peer review by surveyors who apply the same standards and who should arrive at the same conclusion.

The JCAHO has begun to apply technology to the process of scoring. It has developed programmes which can be run on laptop computers which the surveyors will use to enter scores as they work through their survey. They will also be able to enter narrative descriptions.

The JCAHO and the CCHFA have been revising their standards to reduce the number. The JCAHO in particular has been criticized for being too bureaucratic and that it imposes an excessive burden of paper work on those being accredited (Dunea 1982). Here in a sense the JCAHO is caught in a dilemma common to all regulatory systems. If national standards are to be maintained across 6,700 hospitals, then it is clear that the scope for discretion should be limited: that is, that the surveyors should be constrained when making their judgements by having stringent criteria for scoring the performance of hospitals.

Chapter 1 contrasted the different approaches of the American CHAP accreditation system and the JCAHO. The CHAP has random spot checks, whereas the JCAHO and indeed all the other accreditation systems involve a pre-planned survey visit for which the hospital prepared in advance. The supporters of the former view suggest that the surveyors ought to examine the hospital as it runs whereas the latter view suggests that the surveyors should address the potential of the hospital to achieve quality services. The former view is becoming more popular – the JCAHO is espousing the view that accreditation should be moving to telling people what care they can receive rather than what the hospital is capable of providing. This is yet another example of the balancing act of all accreditation systems between the demands of the wider public and the hospitals who pay for their services.

The time between the surveys is also a sensitive issue. A three year cycle is common but again is this too long to ensure that patients are receiving good service? The hospitals in general do not like reviews to occur close together. For example, the HAP experience suggested that a number who had been awarded a one year accreditation status felt that no sooner had they received the results of one survey than the preparation for the next visit started. However, the ACHS is concerned that the introduction of a five year accreditation award may be leaving a hospital unsurveyed for too long a period. The accreditation gradings are often designed to reward a hospital by extending the period between surveys. The most common complaint from those who had only received one year's accreditation in the HAP scheme was that it was an expensive process if it was going to be repeated every year. A two year accreditation status effectively halved the annual bill for the survey. Like other accreditation systems, the HAP has developed what it has termed focused surveys. Three or four issues, identified by the surveyors, which were felt to be of concern to the board are re-examined after a six month period. This additional review allows hospitals the opportunity to make good deficiencies and still be awarded accreditation status. The JCAHO has a similar category of conditional accreditation which requires a health care organization to achieve compliance within a limited time period.

The process of accreditation tends not to be cheap. When run by not-for-profit organizations, there is a need to cover not only costs, but also future new developments. The JCAHO and the CCHFA are required by their boards to hold significant reserves. As mentioned earlier, the extent to which an accreditation organization can sustain its market position will depend upon its internal resources. The JCAHO has a staff of 500 and an annual budget of $US100 million. The ACHS has a staff of 40. The King's Fund a staff of 35.

The method of payment for surveys also varies. In some systems, the payment is made by surveyor days. The providing organization can in theory select the number of survey days it buys and the number of surveyors allocated will determine the total length of the survey. The pricing policies raise a number of difficulties. First organizations object to paying for surveys which produce unsatisfactory results. Because of the grading structure, which gives one, two or a number of years' accreditation, a poor organization effectively has to pay a financial penalty by incurring a more frequent survey fee. In Canada the fee structure was changed to resist accusations that the accreditation awards were being reduced in order to raise extra income. This change also enabled the separation of the funding of the Council from the surveys of facilities. The CCHFA now charges an annual fee, calculated on the basis of the size of the participating organization and a fee which covers the cost of the survey per surveyor day.

This shows the curious relationship of accreditation with its 'customers'. Fee paying customers frequently feel that they should control what they are buying. For this reason, the standards promoted by such accreditation systems have to be muted to meet the limitations of the marketplace. Unacceptably high standards, which incur fines on non-compliance, will usually put off fee-paying customers.

All accreditation systems suffer from the potential criticism that their impact ends at the end of the survey. In order to sustain their value, and indeed their influence, there is a need to encourage participants to continue to use the standards and to perceive benefits from them. This is not only in line with the models of continuous quality improvement. It also makes good commercial sense. Although the Canadian and the JCAHO have the built-in advantage of a limited life expectancy of the accreditation status, and governmental expectations that participating organizations will continue to seek accreditation, they are still looking for ways to ensure their market domination. The JCAHO has well developed

customer services with telephone lines to answer queries on standards, and consultancy services to help organizations develop practice. The advantage of the JCAHO computer program is that it can
be given to health services to check continuously their own status
over time, and ties the participating organizations into the accreditation process. They are not given much time and opportunity to
seek other quality control systems. This bond is made stronger if the
standards are changing rapidly. The Canadians equally are investigating ways of encouraging participants to keep accreditation at the
forefront of their minds, by encouraging them to keep checking
their performance against standards. Indeed the design of the new
standards is intended to make it nearly impossible for a health care
facility to begin preparations for the survey within a few months of
the survey.

One of the difficulties faced by an accreditation system is to
ensure that the recommendations made, if they are serious statements about organizational quality, should be acted upon by the
participating institution. Again it is therefore very important that
the recommendations should be implementable. And if they require capital expenditure, few health service organizations can find
resources to meet these needs. So the recommendations need to be
scrutinized for acceptability. On the other hand, if the purpose of
accreditation is to ensure improvement in standards, the accreditors
cannot simply ignore organizational deficiencies because the institution does not want to hear them. For this reason, accreditation
bodies normally demand that the final outcome and report is the
responsibility of the board which provides a protective umbrella for
the surveyors in their decision making and can decide, according to
the policy of the accreditation scheme the appropriate outcome.

But this approach brings a number of difficulties. There is a
debate as to whether reports should be written in situ or examined
by the boards before the assessment. A common failing of accreditation systems is the problematic relationship between the requirement for some feedback to the client organization before the
surveyors leave, and the need to ensure that the final report reflects
what is said at the feedback. As noted earlier, the JCAHO has
resolved this by introducing laptop computers which enable the
report to be produced before the surveyors leave the site. However,
the experience of other accreditation systems is that there are
dangers in this process unless it is very well controlled. Trent
Community Hospital scheme found that its surveyors were inform-
ing surveyed organizations of their accreditation status before the

board had ratified the conclusions. When the board awarded a different status to the one the organization had been told to expect the organizations were understandably aggrieved.

Associated with this is the time that elapses between the survey and the completion of the report. Sustaining staff interest in something which has been forgotten is difficult. The JCAHO has a target of 60 days elapsed time, which is a considerable improvement on their previous efforts of five or six months. It is a truism, but the greater the number of organizations which participate in the process, the greater the amount of board time needed to review the surveyors' decisions will be. The JCAHO, with its extensive coverage of USA hospitals and other health care providers has moved away from such extensive reliance on the board, and has a complex internal organization to review accreditation decisions.

There is also an issue surrounding the time between the survey and the identification of deficiencies, and the follow up to check on whether a hospital has implemented the recommendations. In the educational philosophy, such as that followed by the JCAHO, it is argued that hospitals need time to develop and implement solutions. But this was found to be unacceptable to the Health Care Financing Administration who, in the summer of 1989, criticized the JCAHO's 15 month time lag between survey and follow-up. The JCAHO was forced to respond by reducing the time of follow up and finding other ways of implementing checks on hospital performance (Bankhead 1990).

The value of the accreditation status to the accrediting organization, however it is perceived and used, cannot be underestimated. The King's Fund is the one system which employs all the processes of accreditation but does not award an accreditation status. As a consequence, the King's Fund has less committed participants and fewer powers to 'tie' them in. Interviews with chief executives in the acute units have shown less commitment to the continuing process: 'We will wait to see if something better comes along. We are not sure the King's Fund is the answer.' The chief executives of NHS Trusts have less reason to be worried about the lack of accreditation status. At present, criticism by an accreditation body is not going to affect them financially, nor in terms of public perceptions. The effect is that the accreditation systems are seen as something to be bought 'so long as they are useful'. And the UK schemes therefore have a less secure future and operate in a more demanding and competitive environment.

Without sanctions accreditation has no teeth. But in the health care sector, 'the art of effective external control often involves trying to improve service provision while still ensuring that the services remain widely available' (Vladeck 1988). Sanctions which result in the closure of providing organizations merely deprive the public of a necessary service, unless the market has spare capacity, and even so may force existing users to bear high and emotionally painful switching costs. Assuming that patients have invested an amount of time and effort in choosing a provider, or gain some form of psychological reassurance from knowing that the provider is there, there must be costs attached to closure of institutions. The alternative is the sanction of fining organizations, but as pointed out elsewhere, all this does is to ultimately deprive patients of resources which could be spent on them. And, the threat of non-accredit-ation, particularly after a referral decision, ensures that organiz-ations take notice of the recommendations. The King's Fund, without the accreditation decision faces more difficulties in per-suading hospitals to act upon the recommendations.

However, dealing with failure presents some interesting mana-gerial and social problems. The Japanese are developing a system of accreditation. Within their culture, to fail is unacceptable. There is therefore no discussion of failure within their systems. The JCAHO and the CCHFA both acknowledge the need for health care organizations to appeal against the status awarded. In the case of the CCHFA a formal application for review must be made which must outline clearly and in detail why the review is justified. The review is heard by a committee of three board members, selected by the Council and the appellant is charged for the costs of the hearing. The JCAHO, with its more complex method of scoring and determining accreditation status has a more complex appeal process.

As a consequence of the harsh effects of failing an organization, the JCAHO has been criticized for being too lax with its approach. It is inevitably hard to penalize an organization which will cease to exist on this outcome. Furthermore, it is not sensible to put one of your customers out of business as they will no longer be in a position to buy your services. This unease and reluctance to share infor-mation makes an interesting comparison with the recent develop-ments of the JCAHO who are moving towards more and more public information. The JCAHO is responding to greater consumer pressure to inform public choice.

THE PUBLICNESS OF INFORMATION

It is not only the JCAHO which is being forced to make its findings public. In Canada, the fact that a hospital has been through the process is made public. In Australia the whole process and the outcome remains confidential to the facility involved. The publicness of the information gleaned from a survey visit is one with which all accreditation systems are forced to grapple. Traditionally, providers appear to have been very reluctant to share information with consumers, well demonstrated by the anecdote of the burning of the very first USA survey results in 1919 (see Chapter 1). On 12 October 1988, the *Wall Street Journal* reported the continuing reluctance of the JCAHO to share information with the public.

> A policy of keeping hospital deficiencies under tight wraps reflects the spirit of cooperation . . . without the promise of confidentiality, the JCAHO argues, hospitals wouldn't voluntarily agree to open their private records to outsiders.
>
> (Bogdanich 1988)

The article caused public outcry, resulting in pressure being brought to bear on the JCAHO to provide selected survey data to the Health Care Financing Administration, who may then choose to make the information public. The accreditation systems are caught between the need to meet the needs of their clients for confidential audit and review, and the public who wish to know about the quality of the health care system to which they are exposed.

The status conferred is traditionally not disclosed. But where pressure is brought to bear, usually by public bodies demanding accountability (as seen in the USA and Canada) to make information available to the public, there are problems in determining how much information should be passed on. One concern is whether the public is educated in understanding the process and therefore can grasp the significance of the status awarded. In the USA it has been claimed that the public has been led to place too much faith in the accreditation process assuming that it offers a guarantee of safety and good practice (Bogdanich 1988). The simple pass/fail indicator was not considered to be enough. In 1994 USA health care consumers will have access to performance information for the first time nationwide (Bergman 1993b). An alternative would be to make the reports from the survey available to public regulatory bodies who could use this to reassure themselves that standards are being met. If this should occur, accreditation would move significantly from self-regulation towards public regulation.

The JCAHO has evolved a public disclosure document which contains the absolute score of the hospital, a comparison with all other hospitals, bar charts to demonstrate the relative performance about certain aspects of care such as assessment of patient needs, medication use, operative and other procedures, and department specific information. In 1995 the format will be changed to give a different picture which cuts across departmental performance. Public disclosure is a curious development for an organization which claims its primary role is in serving its main client, the participating organization. One explanation of this behaviour is that the JCAHO, although still aware of the needs of client organizations, is in fact beginning to respond to the need to position itself as a protector of consumer and public interest. The publication of findings reinforces its position as the arbiter of good quality. It is beginning to build a public constituency by providing the public with information. The CCHFA has not followed this route, keeping its reports confidential. However, provincial governments have begun requesting them from participating health care facilities. Not surprisingly, the information has a habit of finding its way into the public domain where there is sufficient public interest.

Accreditation systems frequently perceive it as their responsibility to respond to any public criticism of health service performance. The CCHFA and the JCAHO will resurvey if there are grounds to believe that there has been a serious breach of accreditation standards. This is a necessary procedure to protect the value of accreditation status. As with any award which lasts for any length of time, the awarding body is always vulnerable to a decline in standards which occurs between surveyor visits. This is especially true if meeting the standards requires continuous effort. Organizations may work hard to achieve the standards at the time of survey only to revert to old practices and behaviours after the event. The JCAHO also invites members of the public to write in with their views about compliance with standards. In 1996 it will require a hospital, through the medium of local newspapers, to place an advertisement asking members of the public to comment on its performance. This is a new development in the assessment of hospital performance. It exposes the hospital to criticism from actual and potential patients for judgement against the standards.

THE SCOPE OF ACCREDITATION

The number of services covered by accreditation is also growing as the accreditation systems seek to grow their markets of potential customers. The JCAHO now covers home health, ambulatory surgery and other services. The Canadian system is also developing into other areas. This is partly due to a form of protectionism. If they do not, someone else will. In addition, if growth is the objective, and for a privately run organization it is unlikely that growth is not on the agenda, growth can only really occur by moving into new market sectors. The JCAHO is finding that they have covered such a large proportion of the market of acute hospitals that they are being forced to look elsewhere for new customers. The Canadian system is certainly expanding under its own growth imperative, but it is also under considerable pressure to adapt and change because of changes occurring in the structure of the Canadian health care system. Regionalization of health services within the provinces is resulting in new forms of health care organizations which combine all types of care under single executive boards. To be able to offer comprehensive coverage of the Canadian health care system, the CCHFA is forced to expand into these newer areas. It is also possible that if the CCHFA did not acknowledge new areas for development, the professionals would establish their own. It may well be that part of the reason for the proliferation of systems in the UK is because there was no one body which could move fast enough to fill the demand for accreditation.

Perceptions of the structure of health care and its organizational boundaries are also changing (Scrivens 1994). This is forcing the accreditation systems to adapt their definitions of organization and accordingly the standards. In the UK, as elsewhere, there is a growing concern that the current structure of health services needs to change. Policy is directed at altering the boundaries between primary and secondary care, and the future of the traditional hospital is in doubt. Therefore, the accreditation processes are moving to reflect these changes and indeed, to be seen to be at the forefront of promoting them.

In keeping with the Agenda for Change . . . focusing on the organization as a complex system, by creating consistent expectations across departments/services, and by giving the organization more flexibility and choice in setting priorities and devising strategies to improve – strategies that respond more

closely to the real needs of the patients and the community the
organization serves.

(JCAHO 1989)

The change in orientation is significant for two reasons. The
JCAHO claim that they are reducing the number of standards and
are also trying to decrease the prescriptiveness and detail of
standards. They are therefore trying to move away from a
prescriptive model of management inherent within the accreditation system. Second, they are trying to recast the traditional views
of the structure of the hospital and its services to something more
flexible. Standards are therefore being written to reflect service
structures and the delivery of care. In many cases the aspiration of
the accreditation system is to track the standards of care provided to
an individual patient as they travel through the system (Canadian
Council on Health Facilities Accreditation 1994).

SELECTION AND TRAINING OF SURVEYORS

The selection and training of surveyors is crucial for the success of
accreditation systems. The difficulty with hospital accreditation has
always been that it relies on the value judgements of surveyors
(McAlary 1981). There are arguments that only specialists from a
field are competent to judge an individual profession. It follows
from this view therefore that whole hospital accreditation is a
nonsense. This conflicts with the view that problems of organization
occur not within the defined areas of professional practice but
between them (Shaw 1982; Shaw and Brooks 1991).

The ACHS has a well developed set of criteria for employing
surveyors, which involves voluntary application. They are then
screened for suitability according to the criteria, then interviewed
and then trained. In all the accreditation systems, surveyors have to
be senior managers, and have to have considerable management or
service experience. The Australian system demands that all surveyors must come from facilities with more than 50 beds. Although
unfortunately discriminating against surveyors from small hospitals
it is felt that smaller institutions would have no credibility in the eyes
of large teaching hospitals. Another issue is the mix of public and
private surveyors. Again this depends upon the national infrastructure of the health service in which accreditation is operating. In
Australia, as in the UK case of the King's Fund, many more private

hospitals go through accreditation than public hospitals. In the UK private hospitals tend to be smaller than the public hospitals and the public managers feel that the private managers do not appreciate the problems of running larger institutions. Equally the private managers feel that the public managers do not appreciate the different pressures under which they operate.

In Canada, the CCHFA established an education programme to develop training for new surveyors which lasts for four and a half days, including a mini site survey. All surveyors must be continuously educated in the changing standards and practices and must keep up their experience as surveyors. In Canada and Australia surveyors are required to do at least ten days' surveying each year. As most of the schemes are moving towards consultation models, they are forced to only employ people who have considerable health service experience. The United States has 720 surveyors, 75 of whom are full time. Most of the surveyors have taken early retirement and survey for about five to ten years post-retirement. There are 120 who are part-time employees who work for a block of one or two months at a time. The remainder are clinically active. All the other accreditation schemes use professional active volunteers. Canada uses 275 volunteers to undertake approximately 400 surveys a year, Australia 250 to undertake 200 surveys a year, the King's Fund 200 to undertake 100 surveys a year and the HAP scheme 25 clinical managers and general practitioners to do 20 surveys a year.

However, all systems are experiencing increasing problems with finding an appropriate number of surveyors to undertake surveys. The calculation is not difficult. The more complex the service and the more standards, the more survey days are required. This can be achieved by each surveyor doing more days or using more surveyors. The more repeat surveys there are the more surveyors are needed. To some extent the outcome of the accreditation process must be related to the setting of the levels of the standards and the number of available surveyors. If there are too many standards, or they are likely to result in the need for many frequent resurveys, there will be too much pressure on the available pool of surveyors. There is therefore, a fine balance to be struck by an accreditation system in terms of its ability to push forward the demands for improved quality and the resources available for it to carry out its task. Full-time surveyors are one solution, but the JCAHO found that the use of full-time surveyors had led to loss of clinical credibility (Legge 1982).

In the United Kingdom, the pluralistic nature of accreditation is resulting in great demands on the surveyor resources. For this reason there must at some point be a limit to the number of accreditation bodies that can be tolerated within the service. The number of senior manager or practitioner surveyor days required to cover all of the health facilities in the UK is great.

The need to ensure that the surveyors have made an accurate diagnosis and arrived at a just conclusion lies at the heart of the success of any accreditation scheme. The JCAHO has therefore moved towards ensuring that variation in surveyor judgement is limited by encouraging surveyors to undertake joint surveys, thus minimizing the likelihood of differences in their opinions about what they have seen. The laptop computers issued to surveyors enable real-time recording of what they have seen and instantaneous comparisons of surveyor judgement. The other schemes, including the King's Fund and the HAP scheme are highly dependent upon the subjective judgement of individual surveyors.

There are mixed feelings about whether surveyors should be told about a previous survey before conducting a resurvey. The King's Fund philosophy is that all surveys should be conducted as though for the first time. However the JCAHO provides its surveyors with information about the past history of the hospital. This preliminary management report provides an organizational overview which gives the number of beds, the services provided, who owns it, a historical agenda which contains the previous survey information and recommendations, outstanding complaints which have been made about the hospital, previous survey report forms and a medical records listing. In turn, the organization gets a customized agenda for the survey days, and biographies of the surveyors.

There are also debates about whether the same surveyors should be used to repeat a survey. Many provider units feel that they want to show the surveyor the changes and the improvements they have made. The accreditors tend to feel that new surveyors will look at the hospital in a new light and raise different issues. To a large extent this debate reflects the differing views of the purpose of accreditation. The JCAHO claim that they are moving towards education and support and therefore it is beneficial to help a health service organization continue to progress.

The complexities of the design of the accreditation system are affected by its perceived relationship to its marketplace and, effectively, the nature of the service offering to its customers. But a consistent theme of accreditation is where it fits into the process of monitoring and quality control of the health services at large.

PART III

POLICY AND ACCREDITATION

6

THE POLICY IMPLICATIONS OF ACCREDITATION

There are a number of reasons why service accreditation is becoming popular within health care systems. A constant criticism of health care is that its quality is both defined and controlled by professionals. This has effects both upon the ability of consumers to control the health care they receive and the ability of the government or other public bodies to call the health service to account. Traditionally professionals have hidden behind the argument that only they can judge their work, the correctness of their decisions and the value for money they achieve. For this reason they have promoted peer review and accreditation fits well into their view of the world.

But there is a growing reaction against professional introspection. Professionals are being called to account for their actions, particularly as they affect individuals whom they treat. As Day and Klein point out:

> If peer judgement is the inevitable coinage of accountability, given the nature of particular services and the power of the providers, then let it be effective coinage. In other words, this is an argument for opening up and making more visible both the mechanisms of and the criteria used in peer accountability: forcing service providers to explain how they police their performance.
>
> (Day and Klein 1987a)

An increasing emphasis upon public accountability therefore demands something akin to an accreditation system, which systematically explains the actions undertaken by professionals for both the benefit of consumers and the public at large. But the accreditation system becomes the property of the public, or their agents, the funders (whether public or private).

Second, the health services are beginning to discover, as Hirschman pointed out many years ago, that markets are inefficient solutions to many problems. He suggested that the option of what he terms 'voice', that is, the ability of individuals acting alone or collectively to state their dissatisfaction and apply pressure to improve conditions, would be a preferable and more efficient solution. To some extent the JCAHO are following this advice by encouraging the public to say how well they feel that the institution under review is complying with standards. The King's Fund, and all the other systems also encourage surveyors to talk to patients about their experience of the care they are receiving. Even so, this cannot be the only solution. Health care is one good where neither market exit not democratic argument are likely to be perceived as acceptable solutions to the problems of declining quality. To wait to discover that health care quality has dropped is not likely to receive much public support. Instead, methods of inspecting or controlling quality have greater appeal. This view, combined with the difficulties of monitoring professional behaviour, suggest that accreditation is the most likely way forward. A means of ensuring quality controls, on behalf of both public and consumer interest, without wresting power totally away from professional expertise. This may in part, explain why the JCAHO for example, has both grown in its coverage of health care in the United States and has changed its approach to accreditation. It has changed the way in which it approaches the structure of health care, it has changed the information it gives to the public, and it has changed the way in which it deals with the management of hospitals. Furthermore, there is an increasing awareness that the public will no longer tolerate being kept in ignorance of the quality of the health care delivered to them. This is leading inexorably to the realization that both public and private bodies in charge of quality need to make their information available to the public: 'There is no better way to assure quality than to let the purchasers of care hold the providers publicly accountable for the services they provide' (Mitchell 1990: 155–8).

Third, growing concerns about the costs of health services and the effective use of resources has changed many assumptions about the monitoring of the performance of health services. Consumer orientations require approaches which recognize the work of those who care for patients and equally recognize the fact that patients tend to travel through many hospital and other departments in an encounter with the health services. Monitoring the effective delivery of services requires mechanisms which monitor the movement of the patient through the system.

Fourth, management theories have changed the way hospitals are managed. The rapid rate of change of medical techniques, the complexity of the health care environment all require new approaches to the delivery of health services. They demand rapid responses from service providers, they require considerable delegation of decision making powers to those who deal with patients.

THE STAKEHOLDERS IN ACCREDITATION

As with any social programme there are many different interests which may link to different perceptions of the degree of success of the accreditation programme. There are the providers who will perceive success in operational or organizational terms; purchasers who may judge the system in terms of its usefulness to assure them of quality of service or the ability of managers; consumers who wish to be reassured that the services they will receive are of a recognizably high quality; and policy makers who may wish to use accreditation to control the development of the health service, achieve equity or some other broader policy goal.

In addition, any consideration of accreditation systems will always focus on three very different issues: the definition of good quality health care and the role of standards in this; the measurement of quality and assessment of the degree of compliance with standards (however set); the organizational structures required for monitoring and the public policy questions of how the results of such monitoring should be used.

As Chapter 1 demonstrated, the history of accreditation systems suggests that accreditation arose from the interest of provider groups, frequently the medical profession, to assess whether institutions are providing appropriate environments in which to practise. Over time, a managerial interest in accreditation has been added to the professional interest. Managers wish to know whether their management is leading to compliance with standards, and whether there are problems they need to address. In the UK, there are few rules defining a well run hospital. Because of this, there has been a growing interest in developing standards which lay out the parameters of a 'good' institution or service. In addition, there is a desire to develop peer review to gain commendations from peers for good work, and to turn to peers for advice on where problems may exist. This would make accreditation part of the internal management process, offering a series of checks and support for managers.

A different view which providers can hold is that accreditation processes reassure purchasers, the professionals, and the public that the infrastructure of the health service delivery systems is at an appropriate level to promote the best possible care. Again this may provide reassurance to the institution, but some perceive this as part of a wider marketing process. In the NHS this may be used to attract purchasers and patients. But such criticism can have other effects in a health care system funded from public money. It provides evidence of low resources, resulting in campaigns for more resources from the government resource allocation processes.

Insurance companies are reported as being interested in a process of accreditation to identify poorly run institutions. By refusing to contract with such organizations, they can restrict the available pool of health service organizations with which they need to deal. Purchasers may wish to use accreditation to reduce their internal requirements for assessing quality. The outcome of the accreditation system prevents them from having to develop quality assessment processes and also saves having to undertake inspections and reviews themselves.

The interest in accreditation in a health care market may be different in a directly managed public service. In the latter the interest is likely to be generated from concerns about professional development and the sharing of good practice. In the market, in contrast, there are many more players who wish to have information on which to base a number of decisions. Purchasers may be looking for reassurance of intent to assure quality: that is they will be concerned to see evidence of quality assurance processes and will accept any accreditation type activity which demonstrates providers interest in this. Or, purchasers may be more interested in actually controlling quality. They will either wish to assess providers' performance against their own standards, or accept third party assessment of compliance. Market regulators may wish to use accreditation to control entry into the market or to control the development of the activities within the market. They may therefore see accreditation as a tool for doing this. But market regulators are faced with a choice of either allowing market processes to work even in the field of monitoring, encouraging a vast array of accreditation systems which require a degree of control and monitoring, or may wish to control the variety of such activities and have only one overarching system for monitoring standards of health care. As the above discussion has shown, each leads to a very different structure for the control of standards in health care delivery.

The key questions facing policy makers are: how to ensure that what is bought is satisfactory; and how to ensure that what is bought is good value for money? In choosing between services which are similar but not identical, purchasers have to seek criteria by which to choose. In a marketplace, suppliers often use price as a proxy for quality. Consumers are taught to believe 'you get what you pay for'. When confronted with a choice about which they have little information, people tend to associate high quality with high price. In the markets of the public sector, where prices are frequently controlled by regulatory mechanisms, and purchasers must demonstrate they are using public money responsibly, such simple market signals are not considered adequate. Purchasers, and indeed health care consumers, must therefore seek other assurances of quality either from their own sources or from providers. Equally providers are keen to find ways to differentiate and promote their services, while ensuring that they are achieving or more than achieving the required levels of quality demanded by the public and their purchasers.

It must not be forgotten that the impact of an accreditation system may also be felt in places other than simply the organization or service under review. The complexity of any health care delivery system means that an accreditation system, regardless of the focus of the standards, may have an impact upon the wider structure and functioning of the health care system. In theory, it can affect the policy making process, the funding process, the resource allocation process, as well as the organization of health services, the workings of professionals, the experience of patients, and potentially, the health of individuals and the health of the population at large. If the output of the accreditation process is used to provide information to allow consumers to make choices between health care providers, the success or failure of the scheme may be measured in terms of consumers' willingness to use the information provided, or indeed their ability to use it in making choices.

Patients or potential patients and their families may want to know that the consumer of health care will be safe in the hands of the health service. Although most people assume that safety is paramount in the minds of those who run the institutions and provide care, reassurance on this fact will doubtless be perceived as valuable. Probably more significantly, patients will want to know that they are being referred to a 'good' hospital, that is, one recognized for high standards of care. And finally, if consumers are able to choose the institution at which they are treated, they may want information on which to make what for them feels like an informed choice. The view of the JCAHO is that 'with the high cost of health care, purchasers and patients need to know what they are buying and how good it is. And these parties intend to use data and information to select their provider organizations and caregivers' (JCAHO 1993). In any state funded health service, frequently exposed to the carping of political parties about the standards of services being delivered, taxpayers wish to be reassured that standards are as high as can be expected and are not slipping.

THE PUBLIC AND PRIVATE FACES OF ACCREDITATION

The JCAHO tends to describe itself as a private sector organization which works in partnership with the government. This is very different from that expressed by the CCHFA who stress their arm's length relationship with their national and federal governments. Interestingly, the Canadian government has a greater reason to support the idea of a national accreditation system, as its laws require that there is a national approach to health care, although administration is undertaken separately by the provincial governments. The Canadian government, although not formally endorsing the activities of the Council, depends upon it to fulfil the legal requirement of comparability of provision across the country. The Australian council has an equally tenuous link with its governments, although one state is now endeavouring to establish whether it can link its medicare payments to accreditation. And one state makes additional reimbursements to hospitals which take part in the accreditation programme.

There are different interests in accreditation depending upon whether it is viewed from the perspective of the policy maker or the provider of service (see Figure 6.1). In a publicly funded system where the provision of service is also public, as in the United Kingdom or Canada, accreditation by an independent body raises some interesting questions.

Where the funding of the service is private, but the services are publicly or privately owned, the funders will have an interest in ensuring that they are getting maximum value for money. In both cases, accreditation systems will have an appeal to reassure the purchasers that they are being sold appropriate care and quality.

Funding

Public   Private

	Public	1	3
Ownership of hospitals	Private	2	4

Figure 6.1 Ownership/funding matrix

Across the United States concern has recently been expressed that the Clinton reforms would lead to variable quality in health care provision. This has resulted in pressure for nationally defined and agreed standards for health care. This obviously connects with the work of the JCAHO.

Spain, for example (and to a very limited extent, the United Kingdom), uses public funds to purchase private health care. The need to evaluate the standards of care provided is obviously great. An accreditation system which sets standards and assesses compliance with them inevitably has an appeal. Accreditation which covers and therefore enables comparisons to be made across both sectors will reassure funders that patients are receiving adequate and comparable care. The Catalonian government (one of only two territories permitted by law to run their own health services in Spain) developed a state administered accreditation system for a number of years, based on the principles of the JCAHO. The Spanish system was established in 1981. This is an unusual development, mostly because it defies the traditional logic of independent accrediting bodies. The Spanish standards, being administered by a public body, had to be written as legal codes and therefore had to be very precise (Bohigas 1984). More significantly, the selection of the standards required an appreciation of a particular model of hospital organization (Bohigas 1985). The organization of the accreditation system differed from the more familiar versions. The standards originally selected were devised to be minimal which could be increased gradually to eventually achieve an optimal level. The surveyors were physicians with management experience. The accreditation gradings were three years, one year and no accreditation. The equivalent of the board was a committee comprising senior public officials. Accreditation was compulsory for the public hospitals but voluntary for others. It was kept separate from the process which authorized the opening of a new hospital. But social security payments and later insurance payments were tied to accreditation which created an incentive for the hospitals to participate in the scheme. However, this form of accreditation had only a limited life span and fell out of use after an initial few years of enthusiastic support.

In the UK accreditation has an appeal to the private sector because the private sector is already highly regulated by the state. Infringements of state requirements can result in the closure of private hospitals. Public hospitals on the other hand, are owned by the Secretary of State. Chapter 2 asked, why then should the government effectively allow an independent body to criticize its direct provision of services? We have to turn to the Canadian model to understand the answer to this question. In Canada the federal government has to see that health care is provided satisfactorily and it provides resources to the provinces to enable them to provide services. But it does not have direct control of the services – this is carried out through its provincial governments. It is therefore in the interests of the federal government to have a watchdog which removes some of the pressure from the central government for policing the system. The federal government can effectively delegate this task to the accreditation body with no risk of criticism of failing to provide appropriate services. The Canadians also have a law that prevents health expenditure from rising above 10 per cent of Gross National Product. In difficult economic circumstances, where cost and quality are inevitably traded off against each other, accreditation provides a means of securing standards of health care.

The UK government, until recently, has had no means of distancing itself from the provision of health care. However, under the purchaser/provider split, where resources are allocated to purchasers, and providers have effectively independent status, it is possible that an accreditation system could be seen as a means of controlling the quality of health care without necessarily resulting in demands for more resources or, worse, political criticism of the state of the health service.

A growing concern with the advent of accreditation systems is the

extent to which their standards are likely to become legal requirements. The theory behind accreditation systems is that the repu-
tation of the accreditation programme will be such that
organizations will wish to join. The Canadian experience is that
accreditation has become so successful and so highly accepted that
the accreditation standards are accepted as if they are law: 'And as a
result, to a certain extent, accreditation standards are becoming
law' (Rozovsky and Rozovsky 1987: 62). The Canadian standards
have been used in courts which has resulted in them being accepted
as legally binding for those institutions which are accredited.

A similar situation has developed in the USA. The JCAHO has
faced difficulties with casting its standards. The American legal
system, embodying the Bill of Rights and the Fifth Amendment
produces uniquely American concepts of due process, and the need
to define evidence on the quality of health care. This has required
caution in the framing of standards in the USA. In 1985 the JCAHO
reformed some of its standards. In this it was responding to the
application of anti-trust law to the health care industry. This had a
number of effects on the interpretation of and the wording of
certain standards. One of the more noteworthy changes was the
deletion of the word ethical from standards dealing with professional practice. The earlier standards used words like ethical
criteria, ethical pledge and ethical standards. This, it seemed,
created liabilities for both the JCAHO and the participating hospital. The JCAHO in theory could have been liable for promoting the
adoption of a particular code, and the hospital could have been held
liable for adopting it (Kucera 1984). In the case of Darling versus
Charleston Community Memorial Hospital (1965) it was established that, under USA law, a hospital is responsible for the
standard of care it is required to provide under the accreditation
process. This was reinforced in 1972 (Purcell versus Zimbelman),
when a court recognized the responsibility of a hospital by virtue of
the fact that it had subscribed to the basic accreditation requirements of the American Osteopathic Association (Rozovsky and
Rozovsky 1987).

STANDARDIZATION

Standardization had a two-fold intention. To enable recognition of
good institutions and to stimulate 'those of inferior equipment and
standards . . . to raise the quality of their work'. Additionally, it

would enable patients 'to receive the best type of treatment, and the public will have some means of recognizing those institutions devoted to the highest ideals of medicine' (Davis 1973).

In the past, interest in the concept of standardization in health was driven by professional interests to ensure consistency across services (Szeto and Willcox 1990). The search for consistency enables the development of a single unified approach to behaviour, on which the norms of professional activity are based. In addition, providers have been concerned for reasons of professional pride and interest to compare their actions with those of their peers. Accreditation systems, based on sets of standards which drew from the known best practice, provided a means for providers to compare their performance over time, and with others. But accreditation systems have also been used to signal high achievement and good practice. Successful participants in accreditation have been able to reassure purchasers that they are providing high quality care. In the market orientation of health care systems, the interest in standards, and hence accreditation, has increased as providers vie to satisfy their purchasers. Purchasers, whether individual or organizational, want to be able to both assess what they are buying for their money and to be reassured that they have bought well.

Standardization therefore denotes an accepted and expected level of organizational behaviour. But to some extent this runs contrary to current popular thinking about the need to devolve management decision making, allowing individuals to seek out the best way of finding solutions to problems and quality questions which they encounter in their work.

For the NHS the extent of standardization is important. It is not clear whether there should be expectations of uniform service delivery across the country. If not, should there be standardization of the quality of health care and if so how should this be established? Should quality be something which requires government controls or is it something which should be left to local communities?

The reformed health care system of the UK is learning to operate under what Osbourne and Gaebler (1992) refer to the rubric of market oriented government. But as they point out, market mechanisms are only half the equation: 'Markets are impersonal. Markets are unforgiving.' And more telling: 'even the most carefully structured markets tend to create inequitable outcomes'. They are led to stress what they term the other half of the equation: the empowerment of communities. In the market oriented health care systems which are appearing around the world, there is a growing need to tone down the harsh nature and reactions of the market place.

The preference of the UK National Health Service has always been to design tailor made systems, in any area of health service development. There has always been little interest in developing common approaches to problem solving. Indeed this is demonstrated by the interest in purchasers in developing their own approaches to quality control and assurance across provider units. But there is a considerable price to pay for this approach. Reinventing the wheel may be the hallmark of the NHS, but the resources used in such an approach are vast. Rarely do health care organizations learn from the mistakes of others. Furthermore, progress is often slow as each organization has to start from scratch. Purchaser organizations are also limited in the internal resources they have to carry out their tasks. There has been great emphasis placed upon gaining value for money from their work. There would be great savings to be made if there were one approach to quality.

However, the local creation of quality assurance schemes may well enable the development of services which are closer to local communities. Indeed the JCAHO has recognized the need to move in this direction making its assessment more flexible and less prescriptive. There is an overwhelming need to recognize the significance of management thinking which requires innovation and local development. But it is also possible that such developments may lead to radical differences in the ways in which services are provided

ACCREDITATION IN THE NEW STRUCTURES OF THE HEALTH SERVICE

The original model for accreditation systems was the whole hospital – an attempt to define the activities of the various, frequently unconnected, departments of a hospital as a whole organization. Over time, the realization has come that the problems in health care frequently arise, not from the workings of individual departments, but from the lack of coordination and cooperation between the different parts. In short, poor care comes when the patient falls between the gaps between different departments. Hence, the standards have been rewritten to highlight the problems which may occur in transferring the patient between departments and care groups.

But the vision of health care in the future does not lie in the hospital. The pressures and the predictions for the future are that hospitals will become small institutions in which patients are treated on a daily basis or with very short stays as in-patients. The centre of gravity for health care is moving from the large hospital to a collection of smaller service units, with many of the services provided by peripatetic professionals who will care for people in their own homes. The concern remains with ensuring smooth transition from one part of the service to another. But there is no longer a single building containing the various services. And this poses problems for accreditation. If the trend towards following the experience of individual patients through the health care system continues, the standards need to describe appropriate care as they traverse the various interstices of the health services. And the path followed will be very different for different patient groups. This suggests that standards will have to describe services devoted to the treatment of conditions even though care may be provided by the same groups of professionals. What then is accreditation to be attached to? Although the health service may recognize the standards set for the care of, say, diabetic patients, who or what will in fact be accredited? Where will the certificate of accreditation be hung? It seems unlikely that it will be possible to have a universal recognition of good practice for a disparate set of services.

The motivational benefits of knowing 'I work for a good service' are lost, because there is no single institution which is accredited. The JCAHO has approached this problem by saying that each accredited complex service, a network as they have described it, must have a central organization to which accreditation can be attached. But even so, this does not overcome the problems of teams, formed from different institutional bases which together provide the complete service. Traditional issues of territoriality between professions remain. The JCAHO has encountered opposition to its attempts to move into areas which lie outside its traditional domain of the hospital. Home care is considered by the National League of Nursing to be nursing business. But it is also the case that there are concerns that governmental duties are being undertaken by private agencies (*American Journal of Nursing* 1992).

In the new world of health care, accreditation has an enormous appeal, providing reassurance for the public about the quality of services they received and a great irrelevance in that it is impossible to operationalize properly. As concluded in the previous chapter, it would seem that the sheer expense of current accreditation systems combined with their structural inconsistency with developments in health care provision, all point to radical shifts in the nature of accreditation. Indicators of 'what is happening' provided through self-assessment mechanisms are more appropriate for the health services of the future. But is this something which requires the vast administrative structures of accreditation? Indeed is it appropriate for independent bodies outside of the structure of the health service. It may well be something more akin to inspection, or regulation is better provided by government departments. Whole organizational accreditation may have run its course, better re-placed by developments in the training accreditation systems of the professional bodies such as the Royal Colleges, and governmental bodies which can react with power to poor performance shown through outcome measures.

Given the criticisms of the surveyors, their lack of objectivity and their potential to arrive at very different opinions of compliance with standards, their expense to the accreditation body and to their employing organizations which must release them, there is an argument in favour of leaving the assessment of compliance in the hands of the organization under review.

THE FUTURE OF ACCREDITATION IN THE NHS

The NHS has inherited a number of small, disparate accreditation systems. But if the control of quality in health care is a serious issue, should proliferation of different systems be allowed to continue, should the market be stimulated to allow one system to emerge as dominant, or should there simply be a system of regulation of the market of accreditation systems? Much will depend upon our assumptions about the degree of protection the health care system should afford to its consumers. Do we stop simply at asking health service organizations if they are acting in line with current thinking about what is a good organization? Or do we worry more about quality of care? And if we do, do we leave it to the professionals to motivate themselves through quality initiatives? Do we ask them to at least reassure us that they are addressing approaches to quality? Do we ask the professional bodies to demonstrate that they are policing themselves adequately? Or, do we, in line with new thinking, worry more about how the professionals relate to each other and insist they show they are tackling questions about the interrelationship of their organizations?

The experience of the USA, Canada and Australia shows that accreditation bodies can become significant powers in their health services. They respond to a need of managers, professionals and their organizations to have some guidance on quality questions, particularly those relating to organizational processes. The experience of the UK, and all other countries contemplating accreditation systems, is that providers want such assistance. The research evidence from the UK, and the developments of the King's Fund which appear to be a response to these, is that accreditation, with its scoring and grading gives a necessary competitive edge to the search for quality. The only question that remains is whether such assessments sit comfortably with the desires of purchasers to control the quality agenda and with those of politicians who are held responsible for the health care agenda.

There is a growing interest in measures which inform the public of how well hospitals are doing – such as with performance measures, which create performance league tables. The USA market system, according to the president of the JCAHO, is creating increased demands for information from the public and policy makers to hold their health care systems to account for their performance. In the internal market of the UK, the politicians appear to be actively encouraging such developments. Accreditation offers one more such approach in the armoury of criticism directed at the performance of institutions.

The systems in the USA, Canada and Australia are all effective monopolies. Each country has a single body which, to some extent, must enjoy certainly health service, but also, public acceptance of their assessments. The public of the United Kingdom do not have a single authoritative voice to listen to. Instead they will have a multiplicity of sources of information, which may in fact dilute the impact of the accreditation information. Many sources of information, which may offer conflicting assessments, will reduce the public's ability to discriminate between health service providers. And it is possible that these assessments will simply be brought to the defence of institutions being criticized by the governmental performance measures.

Will, then, a market in accreditation systems lead to competition between the various accreditors, all honing their standards to produce better and better measures of outcome, or will competition in the market in fact result in a single dominant player? The history of accreditation suggests that it is very difficult to generate complex standards rapidly. The USA and Canada have spent years, and millions of dollars, developing new standards. The UK systems which are already working, have tended to borrow and adapt the more complex standards. This gives them an automatic advantage of being first in the market. The remainder are either very small, focused groups, or the larger more ambitious systems still under development by two regional health authorities.

The UK has still not yet experienced anything which resembles a national accreditation system. This is to come in 1995, when the King's Fund changes its format to a pass or fail outcome. What remains to be seen is the market, in the form of providers, reaction to this offering. If they buy, then the King's Fund may well have enough coverage of the market to achieve domination in all areas where there is no competition. Certainly the pathology accreditation system has quietly achieved coverage of over half of the laboratories in the NHS, with many more customers from outside the service. It has gained a strong enough foothold to be difficult to dislodge even by the most ardent competitor. The JCAHO has evolved cooperative measures with smaller accreditation systems which have a significant hold in the market. The King's Fund has reached a degree of accommodation with the pathology scheme.

But although the UK market has different accreditation schemes, the only duplicated accreditation systems at present are those for community hospitals, and these have avoided competition by focusing on limited geographical areas.

There is a view, apparently held by a number of managers in the NHS, that accreditation should be made compulsory. If monitoring of compliance with standards is to have any effect, particularly to standardize the quality of care across the country, then all institutions should have to participate. This does not necessarily demand a single accreditation system, there could still be competing bodies, but for comparisons to be made there would have to be a means of comparing the standards and the measurement of compliance.

There is a general view that the purpose of accreditation is to promote the development of services and service organizations while simultaneously offering a degree of regulation of professional practice by a body recognized by the profession. However, it could equally be used to offer public protection by ensuring that standards of health care are adequate. The difference hinges on the uses to which the outcomes of accreditation are put, and the publicness of the information. Again the distinction that must be drawn is whether the interest in accreditation comes from pressures internal to the organization being accredited or from external sources such as a professional body or government. That is, the pressure to take part in such a system may come from within the organization, which makes participation voluntary, or may come from outside the organization, which makes participation compulsory and thereby changes the system from one of self-development to one of professional regulation. Where the demands for participation come from public agencies and bodies, the regulatory nature shifts from regulation of activities controlled by the profession to regulation controlled by government agencies. And in this last case, participation is compulsory and accreditation has become a part of the public accountability process.

Ham and Hunter (1988) concluded that none of the existing approaches to accreditation and inspection offers a model which can be transferred to the NHS. But they suggested that there could be role for accreditation.

The key lessons from experience both at home and overseas are that accreditation needs to take place within the context of clear standards and guidelines developed by the health professions; these standards should focus on the outcome of care and service quality as well as structure and process; and the agency charged with the responsibility should be independent of those responsible for service provision. There is also a need to coordinate accreditation activities in order to avoid a fragmented approach and to be clear about the powers of those undertaking accreditation.

If external controls are strengthened, then it is possible that a national health accreditation agency may be established to encourage the development of high standards of care. While the profession will play a key role in such an agency, this approach will involve more outside involvement in reviewing professional practices than has traditionally been the case. A new accreditation agency needs to avoid the weaknesses of existing methods of inspection and review.

(Ham and Hunter 1988: 16)

There are two separate and distinct aspects of an accreditation system: standard setting and monitoring. These may be undertaken by the same body, or could be separated into two distinct activities. The monitoring of standards is concerned with desire to employ agents to act as quality assessors. Purchasers and providers may have different views about these aspects. Each may decide they wish to use standards set and agreed nationally to conform with some wider expectations of quality. Each may, however, prefer a degree of flexibility in their implementation of the standards and therefore to apply the standards themselves. On the other hand, they may feel that they wish to define quality themselves and yet employ expert agents to assess conformity with the standards.

Purchasers or providers may have their own preferences for these different dimensions, but it may also be that there are wider, collective preferences for quality assurance processes. Nationally there may be a view that standards should conform to agreed levels. There may also be concerns that standards should meet some minimum levels to protect the public interest. If services are provided on behalf of the general public, they should be open to public scrutiny through public processes. In this case, preferences of purchasers would be overridden and nationally imposed standards would be required. In the marketplace too, there may be other arguments in favour of nationally agreed standards. A single provider facing purchasers with different standards may find it difficult and expensive to conform to different requirements. Equally, purchasers facing many providers may find it less time consuming to use an agreed measure of conformity with standards, rather than trying to impose their own measures on each provider.

All of these models protect the professional establishments of health care. But the protection comes not primarily from the definition and the derivation of the standards. If the standards could be designed in a way to reflect consumer demands, rather than those of the professionals, accreditation may be able to change the orientation of the services towards the consumer. Associated with this is the question of who should undertake the monitoring. If standards have moved towards protection of the consumer, perhaps consumers could also undertake the task. Certainly the currently accepted format of professionals monitoring professionals is expensive and time consuming.

THE STANDARDIZATION OF MONITORING SYSTEMS

Monitoring of compliance with standards can theoretically be organized in a number of different ways. Monitoring can be

		Assessment methods	
		Self	External
Monitoring system	Self	1	3
	External	2	4

Figure 6.2 Monitoring/assessment matrix

undertaken simply by the organization for its on purposes, using its own assessment processes. Alternatively, the measures of compliance may be borrowed from elsewhere, but administered by the organization itself. A third possibility is that the organization uses its own measures, but has them calibrated by a third party. A fourth is that the organization uses measures from elsewhere which are also calibrated and checked by a third party.

In Figure 6.2 Box 1 is the form of usual self-assessment developed by many organizations. It falls outside of the discussion of accreditation type activities. Box 2 is the form of quality assurance process which again many organizations choose to use. This again is not included in accreditation. Boxes 3 and 4, however, are forms of accreditation. Box 3 would include the sort of approach adopted by BS 5750 in which internal processes of quality assurance are subject to calibration and checking by an external agency. Box 4 is the normal type of accreditation activity in which external monitoring processes are imposed on the organization.

These two different approaches to accreditation lend themselves to a variety of different control structures which again may be subject to considerable variations in their design. There may be many different monitoring organizations which are themselves licensed to operate. The licensing of these organizations may be undertaken by a superordinate body, such as in the case of BS 5750 which effectively regulates the market in monitoring activity. Alternatively, it may be argued that these bodies should be left to fight out their survival in the marketplace, competing for the custom of interested purchasers and providers.

The choice of structure will be dictated by the degree of conformity and standardization required across the monitoring bodies and the standardization required in the outputs from the monitoring processes. Where the emphasis is on standardizing the nature of the process, either simply for the purpose of controlling the activity, or for being able to compare the outcome of the process, a national body controlling the entry into the market and the activities of the monitoring bodies will be required.

STANDARD SETTING AND MONITORING COMBINED: ORGANIZATIONAL STRUCTURES

There are therefore a number of different ways in which the approaches to standard setting and monitoring can be combined (see Figure 6.3). Box 1 suggests a host of locally dominated systems, run by many possible organizations. Box 2 suggests nationally agreed standards which are then implemented locally, which may generate statistical returns for comparisons to be made by, say, the Department of Health. This is a fairly familiar route of data returns to the centre. There is, however, an accreditation variant on this in which statistical returns are sent to a national body which checks whether they are completed appropriately and on the basis of this

Standards development

	Local	National
Monitoring system Local	1	2
National	4	3

Figure 6.3 Monitoring/standards matrix

may decide whether to award an accreditation status. This is almost accreditation by post, or by proxy. This system may well become more popular as accreditation resources become scarcer. Only when areas of difficulty or unexpected results are found are organizations visited by the national agency, to check up on local standards. This approach is currently being pursued by a number of bodies moving towards accreditation such as the Child Health Computing Committee, and the King's Fund and the JCAHO are investigating its possibilities. Box 3 is a highly flexible system allowing for local variations in service development to be taken into account but with some national system checking the implementation of standards. This is the system evolving in the Netherlands where local developments are encouraged. Box 4 suggests a national accreditation system of the kind found in USA under the JCAHO, or Canada or Australia.

There are therefore different and totally unrelated arguments as to how standards should be set and how the process of monitoring should be conducted. There are a number of different foci for the systems of standard setting which relate to whether quality is to be assessed in the process or in the outcome, and this in turn affects the decision as to whether the assessment is better undertaken internally by the organization itself, or externally by an outside body (see Figure 6.3). If quality is to be assessed in the process then standards will relate to definitions of good practice and will attempt to control the ways in which health care is delivered. This requires, therefore, an externally agreed definition of process to which all participants subscribe. However, if the processes for achieving quality are felt to be best left to internal management, then quality will tend to be assessed using measures which either attempt to impose some measurement of quality assurance processes or to examine the outcome of the processes.

CONTROL OVER STANDARD SETTING AND MONITORING

The key issues are the extent to which there should be control over the processes of monitoring and standard setting and the extent to which this should be internal or external to the providers of services (see Figure 6.4).

Where the emphasis is on control over the processes of monitoring and hence the organizations which undertake the monitoring

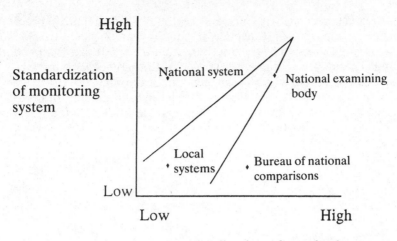

Figure 6.4 Degree of standardization of monitoring procedures and health care standards

there will be a need for some controlling body even if the selection and definition of standards is left to the local level. This body would act in the best interests of the consumers of health care, and the public interest and would have to check the standards used by the various bodies and their methods of implementation. However, if the concern is more in the control of standards then there would have to be a national body which would dictate the definition of standards. This could only operate on its own if the standards were handed down through the various lines of the NHS and would require a hierarchical management system to ensure its implementation. In the structure of the internal market it would appear to require another body, or additional powers to also ensure the adoption of the standards nationally. To achieve both control over standards and over the measurement of compliance would require a national standard setting body and a national inspectorate. These could be organized separately or within one organization.

The most appropriate future is one in which the public is offered acceptable reassurance that health care systems are safe and are striving to achieve the quality they claim to espouse. What is clear from the analysis of the Anglophone models is that accreditation does appeal to health care providers. It has a variety of uses for health care purchasers. It has, traditionally offered little to health care consumers or the public. But accreditation systems are products of the markets in which they operate and are perfectly capable of moving towards a public orientation. All are starting to respond to this. And if accreditation systems start to become the champions of the people, rather than the professionals, the health services may find that they have to account for themselves and their failure to achieve standards in ways which they have never done before.

7

THE FUTURE

The review of accreditation in the different systems of different
countries shows that there are remarkable similarities in the basic
approach and the standards used. The main differences can be
explained by two factors: the use to which the accreditation
findings are put, in that some systems (most notably the JCAHO),
have been incorporated into the monitoring and inspection processes of governments, whereas others have remained as tools of
self-evaluation; and the degree of competition faced by the
accreditation system in the marketplace for quality review processes. There are difficulties in finding the appropriate organizational structures and 'fit' with the health care environments in
which they operate.

But the major policy question remains unanswered. Does
accreditation have any justifiable relationship to the quality of
health care. Can it really assist consumers in their search for
appropriate mechanisms to inform themselves about the health
services they use?

THE CRITICS OF ACCREDITATION

The Institute of Medicine in the USA identified three problems with
both certification and accreditation as a means of assuring quality
(Lohr 1990). First, although valiant efforts have been made to move
to measures of outcomes, there are no adequate and valid outcomes
for the whole spectrum of clinical and organizational services.
Second, there are problems with periodic inspections – what
happens after the surveyors have left? Third, there is an ambivalent
attitude towards sanctions applied by both the JCAHO and even

the Medicare agencies. This they blame on the JCAHO's philosophy of promoting professional self-improvement and officials' desire to make social security benefits widely available.

Furthermore, if the object is to standardize the quality of health care, the accreditation process poses problems in assuring comparability and validity. Even the JCAHO, after its valiant attempts to ensure surveyor consistency, fails to guarantee lack of surveyor variability. Lohr points to criticism directed at the state surveyors who were found to vary in their judgements, between surveyors but also across states. The surveyors' judgements, so crucial to the overall success of accreditation in the minds of the participants, are invariably subjective and biased. There are problems in determining whether truly reliable information about the hospital can be gathered in this way. It is possible to ask whether a hospital has a clear procedure for dealing with budget overspending. But 'obtaining answers to questions like these may help achieve conformity to set standards, but does this process enable assessment of whether a hospital is good or not?' (McAlary 1981: 409). A study of the Australian system in 1980 revealed that 46 per cent of the surveyors' recommendations were not tied to a standard. If accreditation is about evaluation of hospital performance then the surveyor's report is a critical factor. And, therefore, the lack of consistency between report and the framework of standards used must invalidate the process (McAlary 1981).

Accreditation, it would appear, is an imprecise science. It is perhaps best to view it as a management consultancy approach to dealing with the problems faced by managers rather than a tool for measuring the performance of health services.

It is feasible to take the view of the hospital accreditation process being a 'Darwinian-incremental process, or even disjointed incrementalism. This is to accept the process as a phenomenon of development – a start which is imperfect and which – with constructive criticism and without administrative constraint – will be amended, improved and developed into a much more scientific and reliable process. It is more realistic, however, to review the process as random or disjointed incrementalism which again begins with imperfection and which grows by way of continual problem-solving exercises rather than evolving as a result of methodological operational planning. This type of process is almost impossible to evaluate because of the lack of clearly defined measurable objectives.

(McAlary 1981: 410)

However, there are many critics of accreditation who claim that it has detrimental effects upon the running of health services. More important than monitoring processes is the need to engender an innate desire to improve quality. And, rather than acting as a spur to quality, accreditation stifles organizational development of quality initiatives. The damaging effects of external review upon the search for quality are too great for accreditation to be permitted to develop. Public accountability must be sacrificed, by the loss of monitoring processes, for the greater good of quality development.

The majority of arguments directed against accreditation are based upon the view that external review processes are incompatible with current perspectives on quality as something which comes from within, as opposed to imposed from without an organization (Vogel 1986). The supporters of accreditation emphasize the educational aspects of the process (Politser 1982) and its ability to spread good practice by transmitting information through its network of participants. In contrast, the critics suggest that the main purpose of accreditation is not about creating a desire to search out better solutions to problems, but about conforming to the expectations of the standards and the surveyors. It is argued that external review processes endorse what is referred to by Donald Berwick (1989) as the bad apple theory 'because those who subscribe to it believe that quality is best achieved by discovering bad apples and removing them from the lot. The experts call this quality by inspection.' And Berwick goes on to suggest that this gives rise readily to the 'my-apple-is-fine-thank-you' response – a defence against potential criticism. External review, it is claimed, can never take the place of internal systems to promote quality

The critics tend to support an alternative school of thought on the appropriate way forward. This is based on the total quality management (TQM) approach, in which managers encourage workers to seek out improvements in service design and delivery. An interpretation of TQM commonly found in the USA incorporates the theory of continuous quality improvement (CQI), which suggests that quality improvement can only be achieved from within the organization and requires that processes are continuously reviewed using statistical information produced by the organization itself (Keil 1991). 'Every process produces information on the basis of which the process can be improved' (Berwick 1989: 54). Analysis of data produced by the processes of care will yield the information necessary for self-assessment and improvement which must be left to each organization to determine itself.

According to these critics, accreditation, by definition, is inspectorial, the standardization introduced by the standards introduces
rigidities in the delivery of service and the overall impact of potential failure is one which can only lead to a frightened workforce who
seek to prove the quality of their 'own apples'. Even so, most
accreditation systems have been sensitive to criticisms that they are
out of step with thinking about quality. Their prime purpose was
never to be seen as tools of inspection and therefore they have made
considerable effort to adapt their approaches to both standards and
assessment.

THE ADAPTATION OF ACCREDITATION

During the 1980s the JCAHO, the CCHFA and the ACHS shifted
their ground to accommodate the three criticisms: first, that they
were out of step with approaches to quality: second, that they
simply addressed what hospitals could do rather than what they
contributed to patient health; and third, and most significantly,
accreditation standards failed to examine clinical behaviour and
approaches to the control of clinical quality.

The USA incentives to address this question were much greater
than in the UK or indeed other countries. A set of evolutionary
legal changes in 1966 held the hospital responsible for care delivered within its walls (Ball 1984; Darling versus Charleston Community Memorial Hospital 1966). The requirements for the
Professional Standards Review Organization Programme, which
was federally legislated in 1972, emphasized auditing. As pointed
out in Chapter 1, competition has forced many changes on the
JCAHO and as a result standards requiring clinical audit were
developed.

In the early 1970s the JCAHO, using the work of Payne (1976)
and Williamson (1978) developed what it termed the Performance
Evaluation Procedure which attempted to define an objective,
systematic approach to the evaluation of quality care. The standards emphasized a method of reviewing care that involved the
analysis of medical practice. According to Roberts and Walczak
(1984) this led to hospitals devoting their quality assurance efforts
to formal audit studies, but taking little notice of their findings. To
change this, a new standard on quality assurance which insisted that
use be made of the audit findings was developed: the facilities must
demonstrate 'evidence of a well-defined, organized programme

designed to enhance patient care through the on-going assessment of important aspects of patient care and the correction of identified problems (JCAH 1979).

By the late 1970s the USA health care system was beginning to feel pressures to constrain its escalating costs. The JCAH began to place a high priority on cost-effectiveness and started to review its standards against criteria for reducing the costs of compliance to hospitals (Palmer 1978). Similarly, the CCHFA became to be aware of equivalent pressures and began a search for standards which reflected patient care rather than emphasizing the physical structure of hospitals.

So, in the early 1980s all three Anglophone accreditation systems introduced new standards, partly to move away from structural issues, but more significantly, to reflect the dominant view that health care should require clinicians to participate in quality assurance activities. But this new move met with little success. The monitoring of compliance with the standard on quality assurance in the USA revealed that by 1984, the majority of contingencies applied to hospital accreditation decisions came from the quality assurance standards and most of them were caused by the medical staff who had failed to take on board the message of quality assurance as a systematic, objective, ongoing review. In 1989 nearly half of the hospitals failed to achieve the standards requiring quality control systems to be followed by clinicians.

This picture is repeated world-wide. In an Australian survey reported in 1979, 78 per cent of hospitals reviewed by the ACHS did not achieve a satisfactory standard in quality assurance or clinical review programmes. In 1981, 45 per cent failed to achieve the standard. In 1983, 33 per cent still had not achieved clinicians' involvement in clinical review (Amos 1985). The surveys of the UK hospitals reported earlier show a similar lack of interest on the part of clinicians. The accreditation systems were failing to demonstrate that they could have an impact upon the work of clinicians. Without this, claims that accreditation could have an impact upon the quality of health care became suspect.

The assumption in both countries has been that 'patient outcomes will only be improved by increasing the effectiveness and efficiency of organizational functions, a systems oriented organization will turn its attention to processes that are complex, interdependent and primarily team based' (JCAHO 1994: xi). This statement is rooted firmly in the belief that organizational performance is the key determinant of four important results – that is, patient outcomes, costs, quality and value. This was seen as 'the next appropriate evolution in quality assessment and improvement. The accreditation process will be progressively modified to foster the evolution to CQI' (Roberts and Schyve 1990).

This new approach manifested itself in different ways in the standards of the accreditation systems. The JCAHO developed new standards to replace the section of the manual devoted to quality assurance. The Australian system developed quality standards for each service area of its manual. The Canadians began to revise their standards to reflect a patient or client orientation.

There are three interwoven questions which the accreditation systems have been forced to address. First, do organizational processes and procedures contribute to improved patient outcomes? Or second, even if organizational processes do not contribute to patient welfare, can poor processes hinder clinical attempts to improve patient health? Or third, should the systems be rejecting process measures in favour of outcome measures?

THE RELATIONSHIP OF PROCESS TO OUTCOME

Accreditation began as an attempt to assess input by taking into account the structure and content of service delivery processes (McAlary 1981). While accreditation systems remained only concerned with organizational structures and processes, quality could remain the province of the quality assurance programmes. However, it has not been demonstrated that organizational processes do contribute to increased patient welfare. Therefore it has to be accepted as an act of faith, as in 'whilst it cannot guarantee the quality of clinical care, it is a good measure of a hospital's ability to sustain a quality clinical service' (Brooks and Pitt 1990: 1287).

However, we are witnessing a retreat from the authoritarian model of compliance with standards. It is no longer considered appropriate to simply ask whether quality assurance systems are in place. The newer views about accreditation are based upon ideas that quality is better communicated through education and persuasion rather than central dictat.

As a consequence of this, and the new thinking about quality assurance, yet more new approaches were sought. Both the CCHFA and the JCAHO have begun to change their definitions of quality assurance. CCHFA in particular introduced an approach which links traditional medical audit approaches to programme evaluation – leading to a description of its version of quality assurance as a hospital-wide programme (Clemenhagen and Champagne 1986). Although accreditation systems claim that they do not promote a particular philosophy of quality management, the CCHFA and the JCAHO have recently changed their direction, espousing models for 'improving performance'. The JCAHO has moved from 'quality assurance' (which defines care in terms of definite endpoints such as patient outcome) to what they term 'quality management' or quality improvement which follows the CQI principles of continuous search for improved quality using data analysis. It is also simultaneously trying to include measures which describe clinical activity.

The JCAHO's attempt to blend together these apparently unconnected, and often claimed antithetical concepts, into one approach to quality is made possible by the development of its own philosophy of CQI. The changes in direction preceded the adoption of CQI. A year or so after the 'Agenda for Change' was formulated, the JCAHO became aware of the first applications of CQI in the health care field (Berman, Benes and Carol 1992). This provided a context for the 'Agenda for Change', rather than driving the new thinking. As a consequence, the JCAHO adapted the concept of CQI to meet its own needs. The Chief Executive claimed that CQI could be contrasted with total quality management which suggested that there might be a single management structure in which all this change could occur (O'Leary 1991). CQI would permit more flexibility in management approaches.

> The movement towards function and performance support continuous improvement in many ways. With the reduction of the standards' prescriptiveness, hospitals have greater freedom to attend to those issues that matter most to their organizations and to be more innovative in addressing those issues. The removal of structural barriers fosters organisation-wide awareness of the similarities among departments/services, encouraging the development of a common language. For example, by focusing on common processes to measure and improve the organization's performance of important functions, staff members are encouraged to use statistical process control techniques. When a work team is created to measure a process over time and learns how to use statistical process control procedures, all members of that team will learn the 'language' or vocabulary specific to their team's activities. In sharing their

findings with other staff, additional people will understand this language and begin using it relative to performance improvement.

The development of a common language in turn opens doors to new opportunities for collaboration, creating a stronger sense of shared purpose. And it enables departments/services to learn from each other and to adapt resources and systems developed elsewhere in the organization to their own needs rather than 'reinventing the wheel'.

(JCAHO 1994: xiii)

Second, their definition of CQI avoided the need to define benchmarks or performance specifications – so antithetical to accreditation systems.

For example, the monitoring and evaluation process involves the identification of indicators and establishment of thresholds but unlike thresholds, specifications contain no arbitrary level of acceptable performance. For example, an indicator with a threshold might be 'ventilator associated pneumonia rate less than six per 1,000 ventilator days; the comparable CQI specification might be: there will be no ventilator associated pneumonias.

(Decker 1992: 491)

The theory of continuous quality improvement holds that there are two different and unrelated causes of quality problems. Process or systemic causes have three characteristics (Kritchevsky and Simmons 1991). First, systemic problems arise because there are flaws in the prescribed processes which are repeated every time the process occurs. Second, if everyone is applying the same rules and procedures, although there may be fluctuations over time, the probability of both good and bad outcomes will be the same over time. Third, because of the complexity of systems, 'levels of quality will vary from time to time and from person to person by chance alone' (Kritchevsky and Simmons 1991). These can be contrasted with what are termed extra-systemic problems which will cluster by person, place and time. Most quality programmes tend to concentrate on looking for the extra-systemic causes of fluctuations in quality. They focus on identifying the individuals who get things wrong or who breach current professional practice (Lohr and Schroeder 1990). However, it would seem likely that more can be gained from looking into the systemic or structural causes of poor quality. And this is the essence of accreditation and continuous quality improvement.

The JCAHO, in developing clinical performance indicators, has moved towards the model of systemic problems. The significant feature of CQI is the monitoring of the system to ensure that no new external causes of system failure are introduced. In monitoring, comparisons are made between current and past experience, hence the emphasis on developing statistical indicators.

The JCAHO has also been forced to include some reference to sentinel events. These place patients at unacceptable risk and must be tackled rapidly. CQI, it is claimed, is unable to detect such deviations from acceptable standards (Kritchevsky and Simmons 1991). Sentinel events need to be addressed in conjunction with clinical practice guidelines, or protocols as they are becoming better known, to determine the appropriateness of care.

The JCAHO is therefore beginning to develop an approach which challenges existing processes of peer review, which operate by treating all problems as extra-systemic, or external to the ordinary operating processes, by encouraging processes which involve systemic review. The ACHS on health service accreditation, for example, has highlighted this distinction by reserving the term peer review to refer to all the formal methods of evaluating patient care (as defined by the Australian Medical Association) and has adopted the term clinical review 'in an attempt to emphasize the significance of evaluating the quality and appropriateness of clinical care' (Anderson 1985: 44). Peer review operates to identify breaches of professional practice, lay the blame at the door of individuals, and to apply disciplinary action. However, this is an inappropriate approach to problems which have systemic causes. This requires medical and other staff to participate in problem solving groups, composed of those actually performing the care.

The introduction of clinical performance measures, raises some fundamental questions about the functioning of the accreditation system. Not only because it demands much of the health care system but it changes the nature of the accreditation process. The justification for the move, provided by the President of the JCAHO (1993), demonstrates the shift in emphasis: 'Standards compliance offer the potential for predicting the likelihood of future outcomes.' In contrast, 'outcomes measurement [provides] . . . information that is current to the present time'. Standards suggest what might happen in the future – outcomes tell you what is happening now. Finally, the USA health care system is being forced to confront what it is currently providing rather than what it might be providing. The emphasis on actual performance is something health services have preferred to ignore in the past.

The evidence cited above suggests that the process of accreditation is changing more radically in the USA than elsewhere as the JCAHO is being forced towards acting as a quasi-public regulatory body and away from self-regulation. In the struggle to maintain its market dominance against the threats posed by public regulatory bodies they have been forced to adapt to the needs of the regulators. Additionally, competition from other quarters, both accreditation systems and state agencies, has forced them to change their assessment practices. Canada and Australia are remaining more true to the origins of accreditation than the system which gave birth to it but they do not appear to be facing competitive pressures either from state regulation or from other accreditation systems. The UK and Australia both came late to the idea of accreditation. Australia managed to find support from state governments and from the medical and health professionals and is therefore developing a national accreditation system. The UK in contrast has neither government validation nor support from the medical professions. In the UK the pressures for accreditation are coming from a different source.

As the earlier chapters have shown, although accreditation systems pre-date the 'purchaser/provider split' in the UK, the NHS reforms have undoubtedly created a considerable impetus to develop systems which reassure practitioners, purchasers and policy makers about the quality of health care. The advent of competition, and its messages about cost cutting have been partly responsible. But whether these are left to health services currently without accreditation systems to develop their own forms of self-regulation, or whether state regulation is introduced, remains to be decided.

It is also unclear whether it will be possible to use accreditation awards in the likely changes which will occur within the organizations of health care. Current understanding of accreditation is firmly rooted in the existing structures of health care, hospitals and domiciliary services. The CCHFA is having to adapt to regional structures within the provinces. Likewise the JCAHO is expanding its coverage of health services. It is significant that the JCAHO has identified the need for a central organization which coordinates service delivery. Part of the difficulty of developing accreditation systems which cut across organizational boundaries means that there is no identifiable organization which would seek or be awarded accreditation status. What precisely is it that will be accredited? In very simplistic terms, there is no location in which the plaque showing an accreditation award can be placed. The accreditation status must be owned by an identifiable organization or it has no meaning. In short, it is not clear who or what is being accredited. Although it is possible to envisage a situation in which purchasers comprehend service accreditation, it is not clear that consumers will be able to easily use the same points of reference.

But the greatest problem is encountered if accreditation is intended to give signals on the quality of health care, rather than simply complying with good organizational practices. Can accreditation assure consumers and the public that health care is effective?

For this to be the case, one of two possible assumptions has to be made. Either it is acceptable for accreditation to continue to measure processes, because there is a guaranteed and explicable relationship between service inputs and health outcomes. Or, the accreditation process can move to a point of measuring and examining outcomes itself. A limited number of studies have attempted to relate organizational attributes such as 'coordination' or 'standardization' to good patient care. This research presents many problems because of the 'enormous leap between theoretical concepts and operational measures' (Palmer and Reilly 1979: 702). There has been little evidence of consensus about what, for example, coordination should be or how it should be measured. The accreditation systems are forced to assume this relationship with little evidence to support the conjecture.

The UK and many other countries which are examining the virtues of accreditation will have to decide where such a process fits into their monitoring and control systems. Although all accreditation systems have argued that their primary purpose is to help the development of health care and organizations, there are few governmental bodies which are interested in this aspect of accreditation. Most governmental agencies see accreditation as a tool of public accountability – ensuring equity across service providers, and satisfying consumers and political agents that correct operational procedures are in place. However, accreditation has failed to support consumer demands for redress using the standards as the basis for acceptable practice. Quality, it is suggested, is hard to document in legal terms (Lohr 1990) and therefore accreditation ratings or standards do not offer a means to consumers for seeking redress.

In the USA, the JCAHO offers providers an alternative to state regulation, for the receipt of Medicare and Medicaid funds. Providers have been permitted a choice between a regulatory system of their choice or one imposed upon them from outside. Although there is no choice about demonstrating compliance with standards, there is a real choice concerning the body which undertakes the assessment of compliance.

As the UK has moved towards a split of funding health care from the provision of health care a number of gaps in the system of public accountability are starting to appear. Which of the two protagonists in the internal market, purchaser or provider, is to be held responsible for the quality of health care? Purchasers are developing complex and expensive mechanisms for monitoring quality, as are providers. Indeed, considerable resources are being directed at the processes of monitoring, and as each purchasing authority undertakes this activity independently, each is finding different solutions. Not only does this consume considerable health service resources, it also defeats the quest for guarantees of equity in quality which might be expected within a national health service. Although yet to be proved, accreditation might prove to be a more cost-effective means of ensuring quality while simultaneously standardizing approaches to health care organization.

Of greater significance for the public, public agents whose task it is to ensure public safety, and for the services themselves who face litigation, is the idea that accreditation may be used to ensure that the services have attempted to minimize harm to patients. Within the NHS, the likely future is that provider Trusts will be held individually to account for their management actions – possibly open to summons to Parliament to explain apparent failings in their management processes. Equally, purchasers may be held to be negligent if they have not reassured themselves that correct processes and procedures are in place. But how are purchasers and providers to know that the courses of actions they are pursuing are in fact not detrimental to the health of the public? And how can they demonstrate that they are doing their best to follow good practice? Nationally agreed standards reviewed by agencies appears to be a logical step forward. There remain, however, two significant questions. Should health service organizations be allowed a choice of assessing body, or should this also be conducted by a single body to ensure comparability of the assessment processes? And should the assessment be based upon organizational processes or, as the Anglophone models now suggest, should it be directed towards measures which reflect clinical performance?

THE UK, EUROPE AND ACCREDITATION

Remembering Ham and Hunters' (1988) earlier warning about the need to be watchful of just borrowing approaches wholesale, it is necessary to consider whether the UK approach to quality is sufficiently robust to accommodate complex understanding of quality developing in the USA and Australia.

Clinical audit in the United Kingdom – when health care professionals come together to review statistical information to determine deviations from acceptable practice – has not been an overwhelming success. It is possible that if professionals can be persuaded to move their concerns from peer review towards an appreciation of systemic problems there may be progress in this area. This argues for an emphasis on the environment in which they operate rather than the behaviour of individuals to make progress.

But JCAHO approach is based upon a set of assumptions about quality that may have little resonance with attitudes to quality in Europe. Øvretveit (1994a) claims that in the United States total quality management and continuous quality improvement are seen as the same, whereas in the UK there is a different interpretation of total quality management and CQI is unheard of. In Europe TQM is perceived mainly as a management tool, a means of encouraging staff to become interested in quality.

An international study of 580 companies, undertaken by Ernst and Young in a number of countries, found that organizations with low profitability, productivity and quality derived most benefit from basic training and team building (IQS 1992). These organizations were unable to use the more developed TQM concepts of employee empowerment. In Europe few public health services have managed to introduce TQM programmes and in the UK, in hospitals which had attempted to develop such programmes, the programmes had fizzled out due to staff turnover, poor resourcing and poor programme management (Joss et al. 1994). This is a notable contrast to the situation in North America. A survey undertaken by hospitals in 1992 found that 59 per cent of hospital senior managers said that they had implemented a move towards continuous quality improvement. The move has happened very recently, 70 per cent had only begun two years earlier (Eubanks 1992). In Canada, 49 per cent of respondents to a questionnaire issued by the Canadian Council on Health Facilities Accreditation claimed to have adopted a continuous quality improvement philosophy (Heidemann, Colton and Davidson 1993). The services reported that they were still in the early stages but were committed to the concept.

It is possible to hypothesize that there are therefore considerable differences in the belief systems about quality between the North Americans and the Europeans. The European approach embodies a belief in professionalization which encourages each individual to strive towards making the best decisions and working according to their ability. It demands management to instil values of quality concerns in individuals. Indeed, it can be argued that one of the main purposes of the new marketplaces of the NHS is to encourage innovation. Drucker (1985) has argued that successful entre- preneurs must use 'systematic innovation' which is the 'purposeful and organized search for changes'. The theory suggests, therefore, that markets encourage opportunities for organizations to develop new solutions to problems. It is possible that this is seen as a creative activity, rather than the more mechanistic approaches to quality review suggested by CQI.

This European attitude was reflected by the findings from the research into accreditation undertaken in the UK. A number of chief executives have felt that examination by external agents such as surveyors can motivate staff to change their behaviours. Simply being reviewed by outsiders signals the need to take the exercise of quality assessment seriously. How this is perceived by the staff is dependent upon the attitude of the manager towards the accredit- ation process. Presented threateningly, the staff perceive a need to change for their personal or the institution's survival. Presented supportively, staff can see it as a vehicle for developing their own solutions to quality issues (Legge 1982). According to Øvretveit, given the attitudes in Europe towards quality,

> the most appropriate strategy . . . is a phased coordinated strategy led by senior professionals . . . in which top manage- ment identifies departments or cross-department groups where there is interest in making quality improvement. Their role is to offer support and finance to quality initiatives which show prospects of success in patient outcomes and reduced costs.
>
> (Øvretveit 1994b)

Quality, therefore, may be perceived differently in Europe from the other Anglophone countries. In addition, the health service in the UK (but the same is also true of other European countries) operates in an environment of few controls or structural regulation. The American health care system, according to Vladeck (1988), is being pushed increasingly in the direction of external controls which are objective, measurable and quantifiable. The statistical basis of CQI may be more relevant to managers in this context.

Vladeck warns that this search for objective measures may be misplaced. The end focus may be on secondary or tangential aspects of service quality, simply because these are all that can be measured. Vladeck therefore suggests that if we want health services to be as good as possible, perhaps we should stop searching for outcomes and spend more time developing and maintaining controls on quality assurance processes.

> But it may well be that the missing link is effective external control of internal controls, whether at the level of the institution or of the professional group. An external agency may never be able to definitively determine whether doctor A did the right thing in his care of patient B, but it can certainly tell whether anyone else with appropriate, non-specifiable expertise to make a judgment checked on Doctor A's performance in a process of checking designed to identify and remedy problems of inadequate performance in a way that does not impose inordinate burdens on either the checker of the checkee.
>
> (Vladeck 1988: 107)

Perhaps therefore a more appropriate system is one which concentrates on quality assurance processes rather than the outcomes of care. After all, to bring this discussion back to where it began, for consumers of health care, identifying things that have gone wrong offers little consolation. Outcome measures predict the quality of future performance (Øvretveit 1994b). What consumers need more is reassurance that all efforts are being made to prevent things going wrong.

So perhaps the way forward is to abandon worrying about quality itself and to concentrate on processes which ensure the correct attitude towards patients and their treatment. The early views of accreditation as organizational processes may well suffice, supplemented by indicators which demonstrate clinical performance. This combined approach would fulfil the requirements not only of consumers for information in the internal market, but also the demands of public accountability. Notwithstanding the imprecision of the measurement tools available within it, and the fact that it does not necessarily guarantee high quality clinical care, accreditation offers a way of encouraging interest in quality within organizations and yet also makes professional decision making more open. Operating through a mechanism of self-regulation as opposed to governmental intervention, it encourages an interest in the development of improved processes. It also offers the added advantage that the accreditation assessment sends signals, however imprecise, to consumers and the agents of public accountability that good practice is being followed.

REFERENCES

The Accreditor (Newsletter) (1993). Funding for accredited hospitals in Victoria. The Australian Council on Healthcare Standards, Winter: 1.

American Journal of Nursing (Editorial) (1992). 'NLN, JCAHO Vie to "Deem" Home Health Agencies'. May: 93–9.

Amos, B.J. (1985). Medical problems in hospitals: what has the Australian Council on Hospital Standards discovered? *Australian Clinical Review*, 5(16): 47–9.

Anderson, Barbara (1985). Notes for nursing homes. *Australian Clinical Review*, 5(16): 44–6.

The Australian Council on Hospital Standards (1978). *The Accreditation Guide for Australian Hospitals and Extended Care Facilities*. Sydney: ACHS.

The Australian Council on Hospital Standards (1986). *The Accreditation Guide*, Sydney: ACHS.

The Australian Council on Healthcare Standards (1993). *The ACHS Accreditation Guide*. Zetland: ACHS.

Ball, John R. (1984). Credentialing versus performance: a new look at old problems. *Quality Review Bulletin*, 10(12): 397–401.

Barking and Havering Health Authority (1993). Internal Memorandum on independent peer review of clinical services.

Bankhead, Charles D. (1990). Performance complaints: bring JCAHO under scrutiny. *Medical World News*, October: 14.

Bergman, Rhonda (1993a). Quantifying quality: experts wonder what's behind numbers. *Hospitals and Health Networks*, 20 June: 56.

Bergman, Rhonda (1993b). JCAHO manual sets standards on information management. *Hospitals and Health Networks*, 5 June: 68.

Berman, Steve, Benes, Robert and Carol, Ruth (1992). National demonstration project and Joint Commission Forums celebrate successes and address future needs in quality improvement, II: Joint Commission's fourth annual national forum on health care quality improvement. *Quality Review Bulletin*, March: 108–13.

Berwick, Donald M. (1989). Continuous improvement as an ideal in health care. *The New England Journal of Medicine*, 320(7): 53–6.

Bogdanich, Walt (1988). Small comfort: prized by hospitals accreditation hides perils patients face, *The Wall Street Journal*, col. CCXII, No 72.

Bohigas, Louis (1984). Hospital accreditation: the Catalan experience. *World Hospitals*, 20(2): 20–1.

Bohigas, Louis (1985). Accreditation in Spain: experiences in Catalonia; a 5 year balance. *European Newsletter on Quality Assurance*, 3: 4–5.

Brooks, Tessa and Pitt, Christine (1990). The Standard Bearers. *Health Service Journal*, 100: 1286–7.

Canadian Council on Health Facilities Accreditation (1992). *An historical perspective*. Ottawa: CCHFA.

Canadian Council on Health Facilities Accreditation (1994). *A client-centred accreditation program: Acute care proposed standards for 1995*. Ottawa Section on Information Management: Canadian Council on Health Facilities Accreditation.

Challis, Linda, Day, Patricia, Klein, Rudolf and Scrivens, Ellie (1994). Managing Quasi-markets: Institutions of Regulation, in Will Bartlett, Carol Propper, Deborah Wilson and Julian Le Grand (1994). *Quasi-markets in the Welfare State*, Bristol: SAUS Publications.

Clarke, Richard L. and O'Leary, Dennis S. (1987). Leaders speak out on the quality of healthcare delivery. *Healthcare Financial Management*, 41(3): 38–44.

Clemenhagen, Carol and Champagne, Francois (1986). Quality assurance as part of program evaluation: guidelines for managers and clinical department heads. *Quality Review Bulletin*, 12(11): 383–7.

Darling versus Charleston Community Memorial Hospital (1966). 211 NE 2d (Ill 1965) cert denied, 383 U.S. 946 (1966).

Davis, L. (1973). *Fellowship of Surgeons: A History of the American College of Surgeons*, p. 489. Chicago: American College of Surgeons.

Day, Patricia and Klein, Rudolf (1987a). *Accountabilities in five public services*. London: Tavistock.

Day, Patricia and Klein, Rudolf (1987b). Regulation of nursing homes. *Millbank Memorial Fund Quarterly*, 65(3): 303–47.

Day, Patricia, Klein, Rudolf and Tipping, Gillian (1988). *Inspecting for quality*, CASP paper. Bath: University of Bath.

Decker, Michael D. (1992). The application of continuous quality improvement to healthcare. *Infection Control and Hospital Epidemiology*, 13(4): 226–9.

Department of Health and Social Security (1979). *Patients First*, London: HMSO.

Department of Health and Social Security (1981). *Care in Action: A Handbook of Policies and Priorities for the Health and Personal Social Services in England*, London: HMSO.

Drucker, Peter (1985). *Innovation and Entrepreneurship: Practice and Principles*, London: Heinemann.

Duckett, S.J. (1983). Assuring hospital standards: the introduction of hospital accreditation in Australia. *Australian Journal of Public Administration*, XLII (3 September): 385–402.

Duckett, S.J. and Coombs, E.M. (1981). The emphasis and effect of hospital accreditation on nursing services. *International Journal of Nursing Studies*, 18(3): 177–84.

Dunea, George (1982). Inspecting the hospitals. *British Medical Journal*, 284: 890–1.

Eubanks, P. (1992). The CEO experience TQM/CQI. *Hospitals*, 66(11): 24–36.

Feinmann, Jane and Davies, Peter (1987). Doves and hawks debate private hospitals. *The Health Service Journal*, October: 1225–6.

Flexner, A. (1910). Medical education in the United States and Canada. *Bulletin of the Carnegie Foundation for the Advancement of Teaching*, No 4, New York.

Hadley, T.R. and McGuerrin, M.C. (1988). Accreditation, certification and the quality of care in state hospitals. *Hospital and Community Psychiatry*, 39: 739–42.

Ham, Chris and Hunter, David (1988). Managing clinical activity in the NHS. King's Fund Institute, London.

Hayes, Jackie (1992). Accreditation in community hospitals. *Health Direct*, 19: 11.

Heidemann, Elma G. (1993). *The Contemporary Use of Standards in Health Care*. Geneva: World Health Organization WHO/SHS/DHS/93.2.

Heidemann, Elma, Colton, Marilyn and Davidson, Catherine (1993). *Survey on Continuous Quality Improvement in Health Care*. Ottawa: Canadian Council on Health Facilities Accreditation.

Hirschman, Albert O. (1970). *Exit, Voice and Loyalty*, Cambridge, MA: Harvard University Press.

Hurley, Mary Lou (1991). What do the new JCAHO standards mean for you? *Registered Nurse*, June: 42–7.

IQS (1992): *The International Quality Study: Health Care Industry Report*, New York: The American Quality Foundation and Ernst and Young.

Joint Commission on Accreditation of Healthcare Organizations (1993). *The Measurement Mandate*. Illinois: JCAHO.

Joint Commission on Accreditation of Healthcare Organizations (1994). *1994 Accreditation Manual for Hospitals, Volume 1: Standards*. Illinois: JCAHO.

Joint Commission on Accreditation of Healthcare Organizations (1989). *Principles of Organizational and Management Effectiveness for Health Care Organizations*. Illinois: JCAHO.

Joint Commission on the Accreditation of Hospitals (1979). *Accreditation Manual for Hospitals*. Illinois: JCAH.

Joss, R., Kogan, M. and Henkel, M. (1994). *Final report to the Department of Health on Total Quality Management Experiments in the National Health Service*, Centre for the Evaluation of Public Policy and Practice, Middlesex.

Keil, Ode (1991). From quality assurance to quality improvement: a guide to the Joint Commission's change in emphasis. *Biomedical Instrumentation and Technology*, July/Aug: 278–81.

Kerrison, S., Packwood, T. and Buxton, M. (1993). *Medical Audit Taking Stock*, London: King's Fund Centre.

Klein, Rudolf and Hall, Phoebe (1974). *Caring for Quality in the Caring Services*, London: Bedford Square Press.

Koska, Mary T. (1992a). JCAHO: safety, medical staff issues hinder compliance, *Hospitals*, 5 April: 46–8.

Kritchevsky, Stephen B. and Simmons, Bryan P. (1991). Continuous quality improvement: concepts and applications for physician care. *Journal of the American Medical Association*, 266(13): 1817–23.

Kucera, William J. (1984). New JCAH standards affect medical staff, quality assurance. *Health Progress*, November: 38–43.

Legge, David (1982). Quality assurance in US hospitals: a view from Australia. *Australian Clinical Review*, December: 29–36.

Lewis, C.E. (1984). Hospital accreditation. *New Zealand Hospital*, September: 15–17.

Lloyd, Peter J. (1987). The Australian model of hospital accreditation: a discussion. *Australian Health Review*, 10(2): 171–8.

LoGerfo, James P. (1990). Quality assurance: the current US experience. *Australian Clinical Review*, 10(2): 86–91.

Lohr, Kathleen (1990). Medicare: a strategy for quality assurance in Lohr, Kathleen (1990) *Institute for Medicine*. Washington DC: National Academy Press.

Lohr, Kathleen and Schroeder, Stephen (1990). A strategy for quality assurance in Medicare. *New England Journal of Medicine*, 322: 707–12.

Longo, Daniel R., Wilt, John E. and Laubenthal, Rose Mary (1986). Hospital compliance with Joint Commission standards: findings from 1984 surveys. *Quality Review Bulletin*, 12: 388–94.

McAlary, Bernadette (1981). The reliability and validity of hospital accreditation in Australia. *Journal of Advanced Nursing*, 6: 409–11.

McCue, Helen and Wilson, Lionel L. (1981). Hospital accreditation in Australia: evaluating health care. *Medical Journal of Australia*, 5 September: 221–6.

McMahon, Brian J. and Winters, Joseph (1993). Models of accreditation in health care. *Health Bulletin*, 51(1): 3–6.

Maxwell, Robert, Hardie, Robin, Rendall, Max, Day, Margaret, Lawrence, Hilary and Walton, Neville (1983). Seeking quality. *The Lancet*, January (1/8): 45–8.

Mitchell, Maria K. (1990). Lifting the veil of secrecy. *NLN Publications*, September: 155–8.

National Hospital (Editorial) (1969) Hospital Accreditation. 13(5): 10.

O'Leary, Dennis S. (1991). Accreditation in the quality improvement mold – a vision for tomorrow. *Quality Review Bulletin*, 17(3): 72–5.

Osbourne, D. and Gaebler, T. (1992). *Reinventing Government*, p. 309. Reading MA: Addison-Wesley.

Øvretveit, John (1994a). Why total quality management programmes fail in European public health services – and what to do about it. Quality in Services Conference, Stanford, Connecticut.

Øvretveit, John (1994b). A comparison of approaches to quality in the UK, USA and Sweden, and of the use of organisational audit frameworks. *European Journal of Public Health*, 4(1): 46–54.

Palmer, Richard E. (1978). The march of history: growing regulations and growing costs. *Hospital Progress*, 59(9): 58–61.

Palmer, R. Heather and Reilly, Margaret Connorton (1979). Individual and institutional variables which may serve as indicators of quality of medical care. *Medical Care*, 17(7): 693–717.

Payne, B.C. (1976). *The quality of medical care: evaluation and improvement*, Chicago, IL: Hospital Research and Educational Trust.

Politser, Pam (1982). Accreditation: chance for education as well as evaluation. *Trustee Chicago*, 35(9): 30–40.

Quality Review Bulletin (Editorial) (1989). Characteristics of Clinical Indicators. *Quality Review Bulletin*, 15(11): 330–9.

Roberts, J. and Schyve, P.M. (1990). From QA to QI: the views and role of the Joint Commission. *Quality Review Bulletin*, 2(4): 9–12.

Roberts, James S. and Walczak, Regina M. (1984). Towards effective quality assurance: the evolution and current status of the JCAH QA standard. *Quality Review Bulletin*, 10(1): 11–15.

Roberts, James S., Coale Jack G. and Redman, Robert R. (1987). A history of the Joint Commission on Accreditation of Hospitals. *The Journal of the American Medical Association*, 258(7): 936–40.

Rosenberg, C.E. (1987). *The Care of Strangers: the Rise of America's Hospital System*, New York: Basic Books.

Rozovsky, L.E. and Rozovsky, F.A. (1987). How CCHA guidelines have evolved into law. *Health Care*, 29(8): 62.

Royal Commission on the National Health Service (1979). *Report*, Cmnd 7615, London: HMSO.

Scrivens, Ellie (1994). *Shifting Boundaries: Possible Futures for Primary Care*, Bath Social Policy Papers No 19, Bath: University of Bath.

Scrivens, Ellie (ed.) (1995) *Issues in Accreditation*. Keele: Keele University Press.

Shaw, Charles D. (1982). *Monitoring and Standards in the NHS: (1) Monitoring British Medical Journal*, 284: 217–18.

Shaw, Charles D. and Brooks, Tessa E. (1991). Health Service accreditation in the United Kingdom. *Quality Assurance in Health Care*, 3(3): 133–40.

Shaw, Charles D. and Hayes, Jackie (1992). *Hospital Accreditation and Risk Management*. Bristol: Hospital Accreditation Programme.

Shaw, C., Hurst, M. and Stone, S. (1988). *Towards Good Practices in Small Hospitals*. Birmingham: National Association of Health Authorities.

168   *Accreditation*

South West Regional Health Authority (1993). *Accreditation of Nursing Services: report of the project steering group.* Bristol: South West Regional Health Authority.
Starr, P. (1982). *The Social Transformation of American Medicine,* New York: Basic Books.
Stephenson, George W. (1981). The College's role in hospital standardization. *Bulletin of American College of Surgeons,* February: 17–29.
Szeto, Deanna K. and Willcox, Gordon S. (1990). Program used by a national home infusion therapy provider to prepare for Joint Commission site surveys. *American Journal of Hospital Pharmacy,* 47(7): 1555–8.
Vladeck, Bruce C. (1988). Quality assurance through external controls. *Inquiry,* 25 (Spring): 100–7.
Vogel, D. (1986). *National Styles of Regulation.* Ithaca: Cornell University Press.
Williamson, John W. (1978). *Assessing and improving healthcare outcomes: the Health Accounting Approach to Quality Assurance.* Cambridge, MA: Ballinger.

SELECT BIBLIOGRAPHY

Affeldt, John E. (1978). The best game in town. *Hospital Progress*, 59(9): 51–4.

Affeldt, John E. (1979). Evolution of quality assurance reflected in new standard. *Quality Review Bulletin*, 5(6): 2–5.

Affeldt, John E. (1979). How will JCAH's new quality assurance standard affect the review function currently required of support services? *Hospitals*, 16 December: 15.

Allen, Thomas Wesley (1991). Hospital accreditation pounds another 'nail' in the 'smoking' coffin. *Journal of the American Osteopathic Association*, 91(12): 1171.

Amabile, T. (1984). *The Social Psychology of Creativity*. New York: Springer-Verlag.

Anderson, R. David (1973). Service and survey must meet standards. *Hospitals*, (47): 74–7.

Baer, Daniel M. and Belsey, Richard E. (1991). Bedside testing: new requirements from the JCAHO. *Registered Nurse*, June: 19–22.

Ball, John R. (1984). Credentialing versus performance: a new look at old problems. *Quality Review Bulletin*, 10(12): 397–401.

Ballinger, Walter F. and Hepner, James O. (1993). Total quality management and continuous quality improvement: an introduction for surgeons. *Surgery*, 113: 250–4.

Bankhead, Charles D. (1990). Performance complaints: bring JCAHO under scrutiny. *Medical World News*, October: 14.

Barrable, Bill (1992). A survey of medical quality assurance programs in Ontario hospitals. *Canadian Medical Association Journal*, 146(2): 153–60.

Bartlett, Jim (1994). Registration under BS 5750: a mechanism for organisational development. *Journal of the Association for Quality in Healthcare*, 1: 39–44.

Bergman, Rhonda (1993). Quantifying quality: experts wonder what's behind numbers. *Hospitals and Health Networks*, 20 June: 56.

Bergman, Rhonda (1993). JCAHO manual sets standards on information management. *Hospitals and Health Networks*, 5 June: 68.

Bergman, Rhonda (1993). Hospitals, allieds ask JCAHO to reconsider indicator mandate. *Hospitals and Health Networks*, 5 July: 50.

Berman, Steven, Benes, Robert and Carol, Ruth (1992a). National demonstration project and JCAHO forums celebrate successes and address future needs in quality improvement, II. *Quality Review Bulletin*, March: 108–13.

Berryman, Joanne M., Applegeet, Carol J. and Belker, Arnold M. (1987). Accreditation of ambulatory surgery centers. *Urologic Clinics of North Amerca*, 14: 11–14.

Black, Nick and Thompson, Elizabeth (1993). Obstacles to medical audit: British doctors speak. *Social Science and Medicine*, 36(7): 849–56.

Blakeway-Phillips, Clare (1993). What has organisational audit got to offer primary health care? *Primary Care Management*, 3(5): 7–8.

Brearley, Stephen (1992). Accreditation after Goldstein. *British Medical Journal*, 304: 518–19.

Brennan, S. (1994). Death or Honour? *Commerce Magazine*, April: 8.

Brosseau, B.L.P. (1977). Hospitals must fight problems together. *Dimensions in Health Service*, 54: 6.

Buck, Alfred S. (1992). Defining quality in health care. *Military Medicine*, 157, May: 260–2.

Burda, David (1987). Insurance and liability: hospitals anxious over payment denials for quality. *Hospitals*, 20 June: 48–53.

Byrick, Robert J. (1992). Audit of critical care: aims, uses, costs and limitations of a Canadian system. *Canadian Journal of Anaesthesia*, 39(3): 260–9.

Carroll, Jean Gayton (1991). Continuous quality improvement and its implications for accreditation standards. *Topics in Health Record Management*, 11: 27–37.

Carson, Frances E. and Ames, Adrienne (1980). Nursing staff bylaws. *American Journal of Nursing*, 80: 1130–4.

Casenova, James E. (1990). Status of quality assurance programs in American hospitals. *Medical Care*, 2(8): 1104–9.

Casparie, Anton F. and Hoogendoorm, Dick (1991). Effects of budgeting on health care services in Dutch hospitals. *American Journal of Public Health*, 81(11): 1442–7.

Codman, Ernest A. (1934). An autobiographical preface in *The Shoulder: Rupture of the Supraspinatus Tendon and Other Lesions in or about the Supracromial Bursa*, Boston: Thomas Todd, pp. v–vi.

Coe, Charles P. and Louviere, Michael L. (1986). Hospital pharmacists' experiences with recent JCAH surveys. *American Journal of Hospital Pharmacy*, 43, October: 2407–11.

Collopy, Brian T. (1990). Developing clinical indicators: the ACHS care evaluation program. *Australian Clinical Review*, 10(2): 83–5.

Cummings, Mark and Freeney, Essie (1985). Hospital accreditation, 1985–86. *Journal of the American Osteopathic Association*, 85(11): 727–31.

Curtin, Leah L. (1992). Of commissions, omissions and just plain missions. *Nursing Management*, May: 7–8.

Darby, David N. and Cane, Lindsay (1987) The New Zealand accreditation. *Australian Clinical Review*, 7(27): 168–70.

Davidson, Dick (1993). JCAHO: accreditation at the crossroads. *Hospitals and Health Networks*, 20 June: 12.

Decker, Michael D. (1991). Novel applications for hospital epidemiology: monitoring and evaluation. *Infection Control and Hospital Epidemiology*, 12(5): 315–18.

Decker, Michael D. (1991). The development of indicators. *Infection Control and Hospital Epidemiology*, 12(8): 490–2.

Decker, Michael D. (1992). Beyond infection control: the new hospital epidemiology: continuous quality improvement. *Infection Control and Hospital Epidemiology*, 13(3): 165–9.

Decker, Michael D. (1992). Continuous quality improvement. *Infection Control and Hospital Epidemiology*, 13(3): 165–9.

DesHarnais, Susan I. and Simpson, Kit N. (1992). Indices for monitoring hospital outcomes in developed countries. *Health Policy*, 21: 1–15.

Donabedian, Avedis (1966). Evaluating the quality of medical care. *Milbank Memorial Fund Quarterly*, XLIV(3): 166–203.

Donabedian, Avedis (1972). Models for organizing the delivery of personal health services and criteria for evaluating them. *Millbank Memorial Fund Quarterly*, 50: 103–54.

Donabedian, Avedis (1988). The quality of care: how can it be assessed? *Journal of the American Medical Association*, 260(12): 1743–8.

Duckett, S.J. (1980). The Evaluation of Hospital Accreditation in New South Wales Project Report Number 10. *An analysis of survey reports*. School of Health Administration University of New South Wales Australia.

Duckett, S.J. (1983). Assuring hospital standards: the introduction of hospital accreditation in Australia. *Australian Journal of Public Administration*, XLII (3 September): 385–402.

Duckett, S.J. and Coombs, E.M. (1981). The emphasis and effect of hospital accreditation on nursing services. *International Journal of Nursing Studies*, 18(3): 177–84.

Duckett, S.J. and Coombs, E.M. (1983). The decision to accredit: the voting process of the Australian Council on Hospital Standards. *Australian and New Zealand Journal of Sociology*, 19(2): 319–28.

Duckett, S.J. and Coombs, E.M. (1984). Evaluation cubed: the impact of an evaluation of hospital accreditation. *Community Health Studies*, 8(1): 153.

Dunea, George (1982). Inspecting the hospitals. *British Medical Journal*, 284: 890–1.

Egelston, E. Martin (1980). New JCAH standard on quality assurance. *Nursing Research*, 29(2): 113–14.

Ferman, L.A. (1969). Some perspectives on evaluating social welfare programs. *The Annals of the American Academy of Political and Social Science*, 385 (September): 143–56.

Gainsford, Jim (1985). All hospitals should be fully accredited: ACHS. *Australian Hospital*, December: 3–4.

Grimmer, Karen and Dibden, Marilyn (1993). Clinical indicators for physiotherapists. *Australian Journal of Physiotherapy*, 39(2): 81–5.

Grumbach, Kevin and Fry, John (1993). Managing primary care in the United States and in the United Kingdom. *The New England Journal of Medicine*, 1 April: 940–5.

Harris-Wehling, Jo and McGeary, Michael G.H. (1991). Medicare: a strategy for quality assurance, IV: Medicare conditions of participation and quality assurance', *Quality Review Bulletin*, October: 320–3.

Hartz, Arthur J., Gottlieb, Mark S., Kuhn, Evelyn M. and Rimm, Alfred A. (1993). The relationship between adjusted hospital mortality and the results of peer review. *Health Services Research*, 27(6): 765–77.

Holt, Phoebe E. (1991). Compliance with ACHS standards in Australian Hospitals. *Australian Clinical Review*, 11: 111–15.

Holt, P.E. and Anderson, B. (1992). Medical record content: recurring area of concern in hospital analysis. *Australian Clinical Review*, 12: 109–14.

Horspool, James C. (1992). Loopholes weaken hospital accreditation policy. *Journal of the American Osteopathic Association*, 92(4): Letters.

Hudson, Terese (1992). Clinical quality initiatives: the search for meaningful – and accurate – measures. *Hospitals*, 5 March: 26–40.

Hurley, Mary Lou (1991). What do the new JCAHO standards mean for you? *Registered Nurse*, June: 42–7.

Hyman, Herbert H. (1986). Are public hospitals in New York City inferior to voluntary, nonprofit hospitals? A study of JCAH hospital surveys. *American Journal of Public Health*, 76(1): 18–22.

Iezzoni, Lisa I. (1993). Monitoring quality of care: what do we need to know? *Inquiry*, 30: 112–14.

Jacobs, Mary-Ellen and Vail, James D. (1986). Quality assurance: a unit-based plan. *Journal of the American Association of Nurse Anaesthetists*, 54(3): 265–71.

Jeardoe, Rita (1992). Domestic services: preparing for accreditation. *Nursing Management*, 23(4): 92–4.

Jessee, William F. and Morgan-Williams, Gale (1987). The continuing relevance of voluntary accreditation: the Joint Commission and its agenda for change. *Australian Clinical Review*, 7(26): 152–4.

Johnson, Julie (1992). CEOs: evolving JCAHO surveys merit high marks. *Hospitals*, 5 May: 84.

Joint Commission on Accreditation of Healthcare Organizations (1985). 'Implementation monitoring' for designated standards. *JCAH Perspectives*, 5(1): 3–4.

Joint Commission on Accreditation of Healthcare Organizations (1988). *Guide to Quality Assurance*. Chicago, IL: Joint Commission on Accreditation of Healthcare Organizations.

Kelly, John T. and Toepp, Margaret C. (1992). Practice parameters: development, evaluation, dissemination, and implementation. *Quality Review Bulletin*, December: 405–9.

Kerrigan, J.S. (1992). Windows of opportunities available in tight economic times. *Australian Clinical Review*, 12: 137–42.

Klein, Rudolf and Hall, Phoebe (1974). *Caring for Quality in the Caring Services*, London: Bedford Square Press.

Koska, Mary T. (1990). New radiology standards reflect trouble spots. *Hospitals*, 20 December: 55.

Koska, Mary T. (1991). New JCAHO report assesses hospitals' standards compliance. *Hospitals*, 5 January: 32–3.

Koska, Mary T. (1992a). JCAHO: safety, medical staff issues hinder compliance. *Hospitals*, 5 April: 46–8.

Koska, Mary T. (1992). Clinical quality initiatives: the search for meaningful – and accurate – measures. *Hospitals*, 5 March: 26–32.

Kucera, William J. (1984). New JCAH standards affect medical staff, quality assurance. *Health Progress*, November: 38–43.

Lasswell, Anita B. (1992). Development of a program in accord with JCAHO standards for counseling on potential drug-food interactions. *Research and Professional Briefs*, 92(9): 1124–5.

Limongelli, Fulvio (1983). Accreditation: new standards published. *Dimensions in Health Service*, 60: 18–19.

Lohr, Kathleen (1988). Outcome measurement: concepts and questions: *Inquiry*, 25: 37–50.

Longo, Daniel R., Laubenthal, Rose Mary and Redman, Robert (1984). Hospital compliance with JCAH nursing standards: findings from 1982 surveys. *Quality Review Bulletin*, 10: 243–7.

Lovelace, R.F. (1986). Stimulating creativity through managerial intervention. *R and D Management*, 16: 161–74.

McAuliffe, William E. (1979). Measuring the quality of medical care: process versus outcome. *Millbank Memorial Fund Quarterly*, 57(1): 118–52.

McCleary, Diane (1977). Joint Commission on Accreditation of Hospitals – twenty-five years of promoting improved health care services. *American Journal of Hospital Pharmacy*, 34: 951–4.

McDonald, Ian (1991). Coming up to standard. *International Journal of Health Care Quality Assurance*, 4(4): 17–20.

MacDonald, Michael J. and McCoy, Patricia A. (1987). Quality assurance – a dimension of excellence for the NHS. *Health Care Management*, 2(2): 24–5.

McGurrin, Martin C. and Hadley, Trevor R. (1991). Quality of care and accreditation status of state psychiatric hospitals. *Hospital and Community Psychiatry*, 42(10): 1060.

Martin, David L. (1983). Health service guidelines: Canadian best sellers. *Dimensions in Health Service*, 60(12): 31.

Meisenheimer, Claire Gavin (1983). Incorporating JCAH standards into a quality assurance program. *Nursing Administration Quarterly*, 7: 1–8.

Morey, Richard C., Fine, David J., Loree, Stephen W., Retzlaff-Roberts, Donna L. and Tsubakitani Shigeru (1992). The trade-off between hospital cost and quality of care. *Medical Care*, 30(8): 677–98.

Nadzam, Deborah M. (1991). Development of medication-use indicators by the Joint Commission on Accreditation of Healthcare Organizations', *Australian Journal of Hospital Pharmacists*, 48 (September): 1925–31.

O'Leary, Dennis S. (1986). JCAHO plans new series of quality indicators based on outcome, clinical standards. *Federation of American Health Systems Review*, 19(3): 26–7.

O'Leary, Dennis S. (1987). The Joint Commission looks to the future. *Journal of the American Medical Association*, 287(7): 951–2.

O'Leary, Dennis S. (1987). A concept in search of fulfillment. *Journal of MAG*, 76 (August): 569–72.

Omachonu, Vincent K. (1990). Quality of care and the patient: new criteria for evaluation. *Health Care Management Review*, 15(4): 43–50.

Osler, Turner and Horne, Lisa (1991). Quality assurance in the surgical intensive care unit: where it came from and where it's going. *Surgical Clinics of North America*, 71(4): 887–905.

Paton, Alex (1986). Towards a good hospital guide. *Postgraduate Medical Journal*, 62: 1063–4.

Patterson, Carole H. (1991). New Joint Commission standards for 1991 require R.N. decision making. *Nursing Administration Quarterly*, 15(4): 65–8.

Peters, T.J. and Waterman, R.H. (1982). *In Search of Excellence: Lessons from America's Best Run Companies*, New York: Harper and Row.

Peterson, Jack L. (1992). Multi-institutional privileging: a pilot demonstration project of the United States Navy and the Joint Commission on Accreditation of Healthcare Organizations. *Military Medicine*, 157: 604–8.

Pickering, Errol (1980). Accreditation survey findings. *Australian Health Review*, 3: 13–15.

Pickering, Errol (1983). Hospital accreditation – the Australian experience. *New Zealand Hospital*, July: 4–6.

Pitt, Christine (1992). A clean bill of health? *Nursing Standard*, 6(17): 49–51.

Pondy, L.R., Boland, R.J., Jr. and Thomas, H. (1991). *Managing Ambiguity and Change*, Chichester: John Wiley.

Prior, John (1985). Quality assurance fosters improved management control. *Hospital Trustee*, 9(3): 19–21.

Puckett, Ruby P. (1991). JCAHO's agenda for change. *Commentary*, 91(10): 1225–6.

Ramsden, Steve (1994). Organisational audit: a keystone for quality. *Journal of the Association for Quality in Healthcare*, 1: 35–8.

Rea, Ruth E., Spring, William B. and Koenig, Timothy E. (1992). Outcome vs process: an innovative response to new Joint Commission standards. *Critical Care Nursing Quarterly*, 15(1): 78–81.

Reerink, Evert (1990). Defining quality of care: mission impossible? *Quality Assurance in Health Care*, 2(3/4): 197–202.

Repullo, Jose (1990). Accreditation of health centres in Spain *Australian Clinical Review*, 10(1): 45–8.

Rhee, Kenneth J., Donabedian, Avedis and Burney, Richard E. (1987). Assessing the quality of care in a hospital emergency unit: a framework and its application. *Quality Review Bulletin*, 13: 4–16.

Rontal, Robyn, Kiess, Mary Jo, DesHarnais, Susan and Reutter, Kris (1991). Applications for risk-adjusted outcome measures. *Quality Assurance in Health Care*, 3(4): 283–92.

Russon, Ncil (1992). A review process for a hospital at home. *Healthcare Management FORUM*, 5(1): 36–9.

Rutstein, D., Berenberg, W., Chalmers, T., Child, C., Fishman, A. and Perrin, E. (1976). Measuring quality of care: a clinical method. *New England Journal of Medicine*, 294: 582–8.

Scottish Office NHS in Scotland Management Executive (1992). *Improving Health Care – A Guide: the National Health Service in Scotland Framework for Action*, Edinburgh: Scottish Office.

Scrivens, Ellie and Redmayne, Sharon (1995). Opinions on Accreditation, in E. Scrivens (ed.) *Experiences and Views of Accreditation*. Keele: Keele University Press.

Shanks, John and Frater, Alison (1993). Health status, outcome and attributability: is a red rose red in the dark? *Quality in Health Care*, 3(2): 259–62.

Simunic, M. (1986) Accreditation in Yugoslavia: experiences of the Socialist Republic of Croatia. *European Newsletter on Quality Assurance*, 3(3): 3.

Sketris, Ingrid (1988). *Health Service Accreditation – an International Overview*, London: King Edward's Hospital Fund for London.

Stephenson, George W. (1978). At hand: bureaucratic surveillance. *Hospital Progress*, 59(9): 50–1.

Stuart, Neil, Rutman, Leonard and Staisey, Nancy (1985). Program evaluation in hospitals. *Health Management Forum*, 6(2): 12–21.

Sultan, Shirley (1980). Nursing audit. *The Canadian Nurse*, 76: 33–5.

Sunol, Rosa, Delgado, R. and Esteban, A. (1991). Medical audit: the Spanish experience. *British Medical Journal*, 303: 1249–51.

Thomas, J. William, Holloway, James J. and Guire, Kenneth E. (1993). Validating risk-adjusted mortality as an indicator for quality of care. *Inquiry*, 30 (Spring): 6–22.

Thomas, Donna Ojanen (1990). Impressions: the joint's omissions. *Journal of Emergency Nursing*, 16(6): 421–2.

Tousignaut, Dwight R. (1977). Joint Commission on Accreditation of Hospitals' 1977 standards for pharmaceutical services. *American Journal of Hospital Pharmacy*, 34 (September): 943–9.

Traska, M.R. (1987). Managed care: Joint Commission moves forward on HMO review. *Hospitals*, 5 October: 64–6.

Wallace, P., Lowi, M. and Colton, M. (1986). Practical QA program meets accreditation challenge. *Dimensions in Health Service*, 63(1): 19–21, 45.

Wayland, Marilyn T. (1992). Issues of research and accreditation at teaching hospitals. *Academic Medicine*, 67(4): 249–50.

White, Charles H. (1989). JCAHO exit interviews: far from candid. *Hospitals*, 5 September: 16.

Wightman, C. (1982). Dr Arnold Swanson: 30 years of accreditation. *Dimensions in Health Service*, 59(7): 24–6.

Will, E.A. (1983). Quality assurance in nursing. *New Zealand Hospital*, July: 8–9.

Williams, S.T. (1983). Hospital accreditation. *New Zealand Hospital*, March: 2–4.

Williamson, John W., Greenfield, Sheldon, Andel Henk van and Tor, Sally (1985). Quality assurance in The Netherlands: Part 1. *Australian Clinical Review*, 5(19): 160–7.

Wilson, Jane (1983). The Canadian Hospital accreditation program: made in Canada, for you. *The Canadian Nurse*, 79: 48–9.

Wilson, Lionel L. (1982). Hospital medicine and quality assurance: the Australian experience. *World Hospitals*, 18(1): 26–7.

INDEX

FINANCING HEALTH CARE IN THE 1990s

John Appleby

The British National Health Service has embarked on a massive programme of change in the way it provides health care. The financing of the Health Service is at the heart of this change and controversies over this issue are likely to stay with us in the coming decade, whichever political party is in power. This book explores some of the directions that the financing of health care could take over the next ten years. For instance, will the Conservative Government's stated commitment to a health care system financed out of general taxation remain? Or, if the current reforms fail to bring measurable benefits of any significance, will the political pressures to take reforms even further lead to still greater changes in funding, financing and operations? Will the state of the national economy necessitate further reforms? Or might the reforms to date take an uncharted path, with some unexpected outcomes?

For the senior student, academic or health care professional this book offers an expert's view of the financing of the Health Service now and in the future.

> . . . a first recommendation to someone wanting to understand the economics of the reforms and the development of the internal market.
> (*Health Services Management*)

> I believe this book adds significantly to the understanding of healthcare financing. . . I would add it to the library in any purchasing authority or provider unit.
> (*Health Direct*)

> . . . provides a useful survey of the main issues which have arisen in the debate about the financing of health care in the UK in recent years. It is written in non-technical language, and should be of interest to health service managers and professionals.
> (*Health Bulletin*)

Contents
New directions – Seeds of change – Past trends in health-care funding – The right level of funding – A market for health care – Managing the market: the US experience – Managing the market: the West German experience – Some views of the future – Conclusions – References – Index.

192 pp   0 335 09776 6 (Paperback)   0 335 09777 4 (Hardback)

HOSPITALS IN TRANSITION
THE RESOURCE MANAGEMENT EXPERIMENT

Tim Packwood, Justin Keen and Martin Buxton

This book is the result of an evaluation commissioned by the Department of Health, that has given the authors exceptional access to the six acute hospital sites selected to pilot Resource Management (RM), over a three-year period. Introduced in these National Health hospitals in 1986, RM is currently being implemented in all major hospitals. It was expected that patient care would benefit from better management of resources: management that involved the service providers and was based upon data that accurately recorded and costed their activities. This represented an enormous cultural change moving away from the traditional hierarchical and functional patterns of management.

The book draws upon close observation of the way in which RM has developed both locally and nationally, supported by interviews with the main participants, scrutiny of the documentation and specially designed surveys. It will provide an invaluable introduction to RM for all health service practitioners involved in management and to academics in health studies and public administration.

Contents
Introduction – RM in context – Project planning and management – The implementation of RM – The RM process – The resource requirements of RM – Benefits of RM – Conclusions and implications – The organization transformed – Appendices – Glossary – References.

208 pp   0 335 09950 5 (Paperback)   0 335 09951 3 (Hardback)